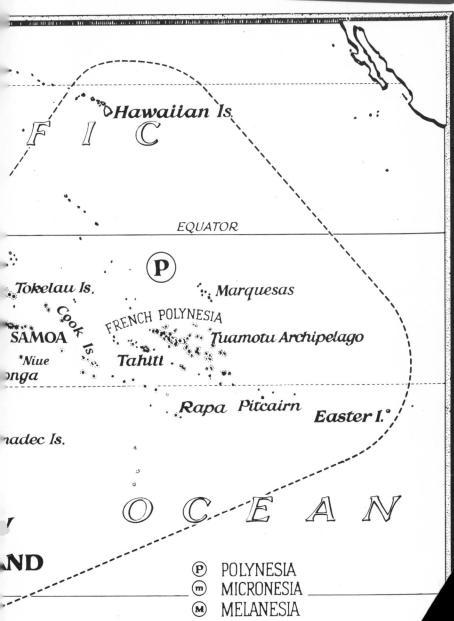

F I C

◇Hawaiian Is.

EQUATOR

Ⓟ

Tokelau Is.   ∴ Marquesas

FRENCH POLYNESIA

Cook Is.

SAMOA   Tuamotu Archipelago

·Niue   Tahiti

onga

Rapa   Pitcairn

Easter I.°

nadec Is.

O C E A N

ND

Ⓟ POLYNESIA
ⓜ MICRONESIA
Ⓜ MELANESIA

Company *of* Heaven

Company of Heaven

GRAEME KENT

EARLY MISSIONARIES IN THE SOUTH SEAS

Thomas Nelson Inc.
Nashville New York

ISBN 0 8407 4036 0
Library of Congress Catalog Card Number 72-4375

. . . in labours more abundant, in stripes above measure, in prisons more frequent, in death oft. Of the Jews five times received I forty stripes save one. Thrice I was beaten with rods, once was I stoned, thrice I suffered shipwreck, a night and a day I have been in the deep; in journeyings often, in perils of waters, in perils of robbers, in perils by mine own countrymen, in perils by the heathen, in perils in the city, in perils in the wilderness, in perils in the sea, in perils among false brethren; in weariness and painfulness, in watchings often, in hunger and thirst, in fastings often, in cold and nakedness.

(II Corinthians, 11, 23-27)

CONTENTS

LIST OF ILLUSTRATIONS

LIST OF ILLUSTRATIONS

PREFACE

There are thousands of islands in the South Pacific. In the west there are the Melanesian groups of the Solomons, the New Hebrides, New Caledonia and Fiji. These give way to the Polynesian islands represented by Hawaii, Samoa, Tonga, the Cooks, the Marquesas, the Society Islands and Easter Island. The people of the Ellice Islands are Micronesians. In the course of less than a hundred years all these islands were visited by missionaries.

In writing this book I have been fortunate in the depth and variety of the resources available. Most of the early missionaries in the Pacific wrote of their experiences, if not for publication then in the form of notes, reports, sermons and public addresses. Church magazines of the period are a particularly rich source of material. The published books of many of the missionaries were based largely on their contemporary journals and letters. A number of traders and seamen active in the South Seas in the eighteenth and nineteenth centuries also published their reminiscences. I have therefore been able to base virtually all my descriptions of people and events on eyewitness accounts. The selective bibliography at the end of the book indicates the main printed sources used. I am indebted in particular to Richard Lovett's *History of the London Missionary Society, 1795-1895* (2 vols; London, 1899), S. Armstrong's *The Melanesian Mission* (London, 1887), and *The History of the Church Missionary Society, Its Environment, Its Men and Its Work,* by Eugene Stock (London, 1899).

I wish to record my gratitude for the assistance provided by the staffs of the Public Record Office and the British Museum in Britain, the Mitchell Library in Australia, and the Honiara Public Library in the Solomon Islands. I am also grateful for the permission of the Melanesian Mission to use material gathered while preparing my radio feature *No Fault to Find* on the life of Bishop Patteson. And to the Wellington librarians Mrs Heather Curnow, of the Alexander Turnbull Library, and Mrs Keitha

Booth, of the General Assembly Library, I am indebted for painstaking work in gathering illustrations.

I cannot end without expressing my thanks to those missionaries of all faiths working in the Solomon Islands today for their help and advice. It is to these men and women that this book is dedicated in affection and admiration.

GRAEME KENT

Honiara,
Solomon Islands.

Balboa and his men. A copperplate engraving from *Collectiones peregrinationum in Indiam Orientalem et Indiam occidentalem*, edited by Theodore de Bry in 1590-1634.

1

THE GREAT SOUTH SEA

Christianity came to the islands with the first white men. The Europeans who sailed across the Pacific in the sixteenth century took with them their men of God almost as automatically as they carried fresh water and salt beef. Piety, cruelty and extreme courage often went hand in hand with these early explorers. Their faith was a very real thing to the devout Spanish and Portuguese: the world was divided into believers and non-believers — the saved and the damned; and it was the duty of all Catholics to convert the heathen.

The urge to proselytise was not of course the only reason for venturing into unknown waters, for desire for fame and adventure and the need to colonise launched many expeditions. But the main reason for taking the undoubted risks was the knowledge that fortunes could be made in a single voyage. Truly, "it was an age of gold, and to the Spaniards the whole unknown world was yellow".

Balboa, that irrepressible soldier of fortune, urging his soldiers on their dreadful forced march towards the undiscovered sea through the jungles of Central America in 1513, desired gold and glory as much as any man. Even Balboa, however, took care to include a priest in the expedition. Setting an example to the hardy friars who were to follow him down the ages, the priest lasted the course. Almost two hundred Spaniards and a thousand Indians had set out on the journey. Twenty-four days and forty-five miles later, fewer than seventy Europeans straggled up the peak in Darien to assist their leader in his awed contemplation of the distant ocean. Balboa's friar joined his master in prayer and then led the company in the singing of the *Te Deum:* the Lord was to be praised for granting them the glory of discovery.

It was true that their way had not been easy. More than 600 Indians, for example, had been slaughtered during that bloody September progress. Yet Balboa and the representative of the Church were not being hypocritical. By the standards of his time the Spaniard was lenient, even enlightened; where other conquistadors would put whole armies and later a nation to the sword, Balboa razed a few villages, and he made a point of befriending the Indians he had defeated in battle, remaining loyal to these friendships. Taking the daughter of one chief as a mistress he was faithful to her until his death, strangled by the official executioner, a victim of court intrigue.

It was this relatively amicable contact with the natives that first brought him to the knowledge of the great sea on the far side of the isthmus later to be known as Panama. His interpreters, two renegade Spaniards who had lived with the Indians and learned their tongue, told the restless Balboa of its existence and the expedition was mounted.

Four days after he had named the South Sea Balboa reached the coast, and wading into the water, laid claim, on behalf of the King of Spain, to all the shores washed by the sea. Balboa and some companions made a short canoe trip out into the ocean, but the experience was not pleasant, for they were driven on to an island by a storm and forced to spend the night up to their necks in the water.

The knowledge of an ocean stretching westwards, perhaps to Japan and the Indies, had a galvanising effect on the Spaniards. By the treaty of Tordesillas in 1494, they had agreed on a line of demarcation with the Portuguese. The dividing line was situated 370 leagues west of the Cape Verde Islands: all lands to the east were to belong to Portugal and the lands to the west to Spain. This meant that in order to share in the riches of the East the Spaniards had to sail westwards from America — if ships could be got into the South Sea.

This was accomplished in 1520 by Ferdinand Magellan, a Portuguese navigator of noble birth who became a Spanish subject. It was the great age of Portuguese expansion and doubtless he heard many tales of adventure from returning seafarers. While still a youth Magellan sailed to the East himself and spent seven years there; and he learned more of the wonders of the unexplored world from his friend Serrao who had spent some time as a wanderer among the remoter Eastern islands.

Back in Portugal Magellan fell out of favour at court. In his enforced idleness he dreamt of fantastic voyages of exploration, but had the wisdom to study navigation, geography and the seafaring arts. Circumspectly he changed his nationality in 1517. Offering his services to the King of Spain and receiving a good report from his previous employers in Portugal, Magellan was commissioned to find a shorter route to the Spice Islands.

In September 1519 he sailed in command of five ships for the coast of South America. The Atlantic crossing was smooth, and the summer was spent searching for a passage through the continent that would lead to Balboa's South Sea. Magellan was unsuccessful and had to winter at Port St Julian.

It was there that trouble began. Most explorers suffered from discontented crews at one time or another, and Magellan was no exception. One vessel deserted. There was a mutiny, which was put down with efficiency.

In October's warmer weather Magellan cautiously left his anchorage and continuing south discovered the sought-for passage round the tip of South America and entered the South Sea in November.

For two months he sailed through waters so calm that he renamed them the Pacific Ocean. It was too good to last. Food began to run short. The sailors ate rats and broiled hides. Disease and death stalked the ships remaining in the expedition. Amid the general despair the undemonstrative Magellan remained quietly true to his faith. Like most explorers of his time he had recourse to prayer in times of sorest travail and then journeyed grimly on.

Ferdinand Magellan. An engraving by Crispin Van de Passe. Frontispiece to *Ferdinand Magellan,* by E. F. Benson, London 1929.

Islands were sighted but proved barren and uninhabited. Then, almost a hundred days out in the Pacific they reached Guam in the Marianas.

Magellan and his men were not impressed with the islanders: a skiff was stolen, and their generally light-fingered attitude caused the Spaniards to name the group the Isles of Thieves. A punitive expedition made up for the loss of the skiff by burning fifty houses, and Magellan sailed on.

He was more impressed by the next islands, the Philippines, which he called the Islands of St Lazarus, adopting the pious habit of naming discoveries after saints. It was here that the friars on the expedition came into their own, and on the island of Limasawa on Easter Day, 1521, the first church service was held on a Pacific island. It was quite an occasion, the equivalent of a modern church parade, with officers and men doing their best to impress the islanders. In their best attire they paraded before a cross, the ships' guns fired a salute, and selected island leaders were allowed to kiss the cross. A larger crucifix was erected on a hill before the Spaniards sailed for Cebu, the largest island in the group.

Here it must have seemed to Magellan that he had attained everything life could offer. Fame would be his as soon as he returned to Europe with reports of his discoveries, and fortune, too, appeared to be within his grasp — at Limasawa he had been offered a bar of solid gold, a portent of what lay in store. To cap it all, on Cebu his friars received almost three thousand islanders into the Christian faith, including the king and queen. The natives could have understood little of what was being offered by the priests, but this did not worry Magellan. Salvation had been brought to the islands, that was enough; in return he was willing to do a slight service for the king. The inhabitants of a neighbouring island refused to pay homage to the king. But the latter was now under the protection of both Spain and the Christian God, and Magellan would demonstrate the efficacy of this combination by subduing the malcontents.

It was a costly mistake. On 27 April Magellan was hacked almost to pieces on the beach of Mactan. Some of his followers fought loyally with him, others fled to the boats, pursued by a vastly superior force. Magellan's demonstration of the virtues of a Christian fighting force and his voyage round the world were both at an end.

His chastened followers, those who survived, managed to reach Europe eventually. Their tales of the islands of the Pacific were sufficient to encourage other adventurers to follow in their footsteps and for almost fifty years there is a record of dogged minor exploration in the Pacific. Emerging from the terrible saga of shipwreck and mutiny are the names of a few who followed in Magellan's wake across the unknown ocean. These names, handed down through the haze of history, can mean little except to students of the period; de la Villalobos to the Philippines, de la Torre and then de Retes to New Guinea and so on.

Presumably the brave, inflexible and omnipresent priests accompanied these expeditions; there are few contemporary accounts. We hear that in 1535 the Bishop of Panama visited the Galapagos Islands. Thirty years later Miguel Lopez de Legaspe founded a colony in the Philippines which must have been firmly rooted in the Catholic faith because an official declared with satisfaction that in each friar in the islands the King of Spain possessed a captain-general and an entire army.

Then in 1567 there occurred a voyage which was not only well documented by some of the participants but also serves to illustrate the sixteenth-century Church in action. The voyage was by de Mendana, and it started from the Spanish possession of Peru, once a scene of civil unrest but by the middle of the century relatively secure and efficiently governed. It was the springboard for ventures across the Pacific and the towns along its seaboard had more than their share of restless adventurers and soldiers of fortune. Rumours and travellers' tales were more abundant than waves in the sea. Not the least of these stories concerned the presence of a group of fantastically wealthy islands not 600 leagues out into the ocean. These islands had their place in the folk lore of the Indians of Peru, and the accounts of the wealth reputed to be there for the taking were enough to whet the appetite of any Spaniard eager for gold and glory.

They were certainly enough to inspire a man of the stamp of Pedro Sarmiento de Gamboa, a man unusual even among the odd and colourful characters to be found in great numbers in the outposts of the colonial holdings of Spain. A soldier, scholar and navigator, he had spent five years fighting in the wars on the mainland of Europe, had wandered about Central America and then settled in Peru to study local history and folklore. He did so to such good effect that he became convinced of the presence, somewhere out in the Pacific, of the legendary islands discussed so freely in the sailors' taverns.

Before he could even think of an expedition Sarmiento had a number of personal problems to settle, the chief of which was to get himself out of the clutches of the Inquisition. It was probably his own fault. Stiffnecked and proud, like most Spaniards of noble birth, he was also jealous and quick-tempered. To make matters worse he was insatiably curious, and this was not an age that encouraged investigation into all areas. Accusations of dabbling in the black arts were levelled at him, he was suspected of having illicit knowledge of secret inks and of being in possession

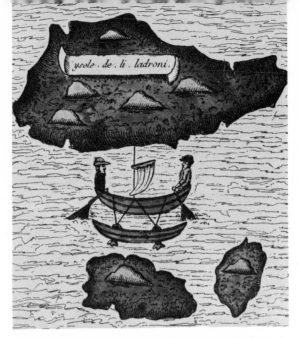

The Ladrone Islands, a group near the Philippines. A hand-coloured illustration in an 1801 French version of Pigafetta's account of Magellan's voyage (*Premier voyage autour du monde . . .* Paris, 1801).

of unholy rings. The Holy Office was swift to condemn and swift to punish. Sarmiento was sentenced to banishment from the Indies. He managed to appeal successfully against this exile but it was some years before he was back in favour.

When he did manage eventually to regain the ear of those in authority he pressed on them his theory of the unknown islands celebrated in myth as having been visited by Tupac Inca Yupanqui. The Governor of Peru pondered and agreed to launch an expedition, but Sarmiento was not to be in charge: instead the Governor decreed that it was to be led by one Alvaro de Mendana, a twenty-five-year-old scion of a noble family, brave, idealistic — and the nephew of the Governor. Nepotism may have had its place in Mendana's appointment, but he proved to be the right man for the job. Though not the best handler of men and inclined to procrastinate, he was shrewd, intelligent, courageous and humane.

Naturally Sarmiento was furious. To have done most of the preparation and then to be denied the leadership was galling enough; but to be put under the command of an aristocratic stripling was the ultimate in humiliation. Nevertheless, he accepted an offer of a place in the expedition — and then went into a monumental sulk. Mendana was to become only too aware of Sarmiento's hostility later but during the preparations for the voyage he was probably too busy even to notice. Two ships were purchased and renamed the *Capitana* and *Almiranta*. Mendana was allowed 150 men to be divided between the two vessels, including seventy soldiers and four Franciscan friars. The chief pilot was Hernan Gallego, a tough and experienced seafarer.

They sailed from Callao on 19 November 1567 and headed optimistically west-south-west. A little less than a month later they reached the latitude in which Sarmiento had predicted they would find "many rich islands, 600 leagues from Peru". For several days they cruised aimlessly but the sea continued to stretch vast and landless all about them, so Mendana and Gallego altered course and steered north-west in search of "some Islands and a Continent" mentioned in their commission.

Sarmiento protested bitterly; he always did whether it be over an imagined slight or a decision taken without consulting him, but could do little other than make himself unpleasant to the courteous and long-suffering Mendana. The *Capitana* and *Almiranta* continued to plough in a north-westerly direction. By December the pilots were depressed and the crew, as usual, in a mutinous state. Gallego desperately staked his reputation by promising that they would sight land before the end of the first month of 1568.

They did so, with a week or so to spare. On 15 January they observed one of the islands in the Ellice group. Natives came out in canoes to greet them but to the grief and disappointment of the crew a current carried the two ships away from land. There was nothing for it but to continue and hope for better luck next time, and that the "next time" would come before the water supply failed entirely.

Seventeen days later they sighted the reef of Ontong Java to the north of the Solomon Islands. But again they were without luck, for a storm carried both vessels south before they could investigate the islands within the reef. On 7 February, however, fortune at last smiled on them and they saw the island they were to name Santa Ysabel. The Spaniards were delighted and needed little instigation from the friars to celebrate their safe landfall by singing the *Te Deum*.

The islanders proved friendly, racing out to the ships in their canoe and coming on board without fear. Mendana presented gifts of bells and red caps and exchanged names with a chief who came on board to greet him. It was too dark to allow the ships to enter a bay lying ahead so Mendana ordered that they lie at anchor outside the harbour. The following morning an incident occurred to strengthen the belief of the Spaniards that God was truly with them on this part of the expedition. Gallego almost took one of the ships on to a reef while trying to enter the bay and it looked for a time as if the vessel would be wrecked. Then, in Mendana's words:

. . . we bore upon our course, firmly persuaded that Our Lord favoured us through the intercession of His Divine Mother, and of the three Magi who had ever been our advocates: for, at about ten o'clock in the morning, after we had put out to sea, and just as we were re-entering the shallow water, we saw about the middle of the main top-sail a resplendent star, which we took to be a guide sent to us by them to show us the passage through the shallows, because we entered them at a part where the bottom was clearly seen and the entrance narrow; and when we had passed them we found good anchorage in several fathoms, and so we found a port according to our great desire.

The star was almost certainly the planet Venus which can often be seen during the day over the Solomons, but to the Spaniards it was clearly a sign from the Lord. Mendana promptly gave the name Bahia de la Estrella (the bay of the star) and to the island he gave the same of Santa Ysabel, for they had sailed from Callao on this saint's day and she had been the patron saint of the voyage.

Now that the landfall had been accomplished the inherent piety of the Spaniards was displayed. This further extract from Mendana's journal tells us what happened:

On this day, Monday the 9th of February, as soon as the *Almiranta* had cast anchor, I disembarked with my Master of the Camp, Ensign-General, and Captains, and Fray Francisco de Galvez, the Vicar, and all the other clergy that I had with

Alvaro de Mendãna. A modern artist's impression, by Luis Carlos de Legrand, from *Historia de la Marina Real Espanola,* by Don Jose y Labreos.

me, and a few soldiers, and we went on shore. Then I ordered them to set up a large cross, which Fray Francisco de Galvez carried upon his shoulders, and he supported it while we paid our devotion to it, and rendered thanks to Our Lord, who had guided us safe to port, and brought us thither in peace and concord with all. Then I ordered it to be set up in a convenient spot, and having erected it, we again adored it; after which the said Father Francisco and the other clergy recited the hymn Vexilla Regis Prodeunt.

Even in the middle of a thanksgiving ceremony the leader of a Spanish expedition dare not forget that one of the prime reasons for his journey was to annexe land for his monarch, for Mendana's next sentence is: "Then, with the necessary formalities, I took possession of the land in the name of his Majesty."

Mendana, however, seems genuine in his religious protestations, for the next day he ordered his soldiers and sailors to attend Mass. A number of islanders looked on in awe; no record has been left of what they thought of their visitors.

If only the story could have ended there. So far the expedition had been almost a model of peaceful colonialism. But the voyage had been long and supplies of food were short and had to be replenished. Bilebanara, the chief of the area around Bahia de la Estrella, had promised to provide provisions but none were forthcoming. Mendana was in a quandary: he wanted no trouble, but unless a store of food was soon accumulated the Spaniards would starve. And there was the moral aspect of the question to be considered. It is a sign of Mendana's troubled and correct nature that he went to the Vicar with his problem.

Father Francisco's reply was considered and just. It can hardly be faulted as a Christian attitude considering the time and circumstances. Mendana had done his best to make friends with the islanders; it was now perfectly proper for him to go inland in search of food as long as he was prepared to pay for it; while it was true that there were enough supplies on the ships to tide them over the present period there were other islands to be sought and food was essential; if the islanders refused to barter then the Spaniards would be justified in taking a proportion of what they could find; *but* the natives must be allowed to keep most of their food and none of their property nor their wives or children must be touched.

That was all Mendana needed to know. He had consulted the Vicar "touching on my own conscience and that of my soldiers" and had received the opinion of the representative of his Church. Pedro Sarmiento was put in charge of an expedition and sent inland. The impulsive and arrogant Sarmiento was hardly the best man for the job, for after a fruitless search for food he entered a village and with consummate folly arrested Bilebanara, presumably as a hostage. But the chief escaped and the men of his tribe attacked the shore party. Sarmiento and his men fought a running battle through the jungle on their retreat to the beach, harassed every foot of the way by Bilebanara's men. Two Melanesians were wounded and one killed in skirmishes. Eventually the Spaniards reached the bay and escaped to the safety of one of the ships. Mendana was furious at this turn of events

but little could be done, for now there would be no more peace
with the islanders of Santa Ysabel.

There was to be precious little anywhere among the Solomons.
Leaving Santa Ysabel the Spaniards discovered and named
Guadalcanal. The islanders dashed into the sea, hurling stones at
the foreigners, but were dispersed by a volley of shots. The ships
anchored in the bay of Santa Cruz and on 12 May, fastidiously
maintaining the religious flavour of the expedition, the Spaniards
planted a cross on a high hill. More expeditions were sent ashore
to find food. The natives resisted and were killed by strange
sticks spitting fire and smoke. One Spaniard of an inquiring turn
of mind found time to note that when a chief had been killed
his men went to a plantation and stripped the coconuts from it,
a custom of the area. While food was being taken by force,
prospectors inspected the rivers, looking without success for signs
of gold.

The Spaniards were weary and disappointed, having found no
Eldorado, merely a collection of humid, fever-racked islands, and
now they were hungry, torn by dissension, and fearful of reprisals
from island tribes. The ships left the coast of Guadalcanal and
sailed on, reaching and naming the island of San Cristobal. Still
they found no gold and little food, and their spirits reached the
lowest ebb. Mendana ordered the ships to be dragged ashore,
cleaned and scraped. All the time they were watched from the
steaming jungles by the islanders. On 7 August 1568 Mendana
called a meeting of his company, asking for their opinions: should
they settle on San Cristobal, go in search of fresh lands, or
endeavour to sail back to Peru?

Then all the soldiers gave their opinion, and with regard to
fetching provisions they all conformed to the opinion of Hernan
Gallego, the Chief Pilot. And with regard to settling, each one
gave his opinion in turn, that though this land was very good,
and there was supposed to be gold in it, and good might be
done there, both in intercourse with the natives and in other
things, it was not advisable to settle there at present, because
we were few, and there were many sick, and there was great
lack of ammunition, and many arquebuses were damaged and
could not be used, and the natives were numerous and very
warlike, and the land extensive and far from Peru.

The friars were asked for their opinion, which was forthcoming: to settle at present would be to the disservice rather than to the service of the King. This decided Mendana, and when the pilots assured him that a fair wind was all that was needed to get them back safely to South America, they set sail for Peru.

Besieged by storms, plagued by sickness and injury, the vessels staggered across the raging seas. To add to Mendana's dismay Sarmiento, who had been placed in charge of one of the ships, deserted, simply sailing away one night, leaving Mendana to find his own passage back to Peru.

In the end after many vicissitudes he accomplished the task, reaching the coast of Lower California on 19 December 1568. A little later Sarmiento also turned up, glibly protesting his innocence and asserting ingenuously that foul winds had blown him away. By this time it hardly mattered, and the expedition, or what was left of it, limped down the coast to Peru to make its report: new lands had been discovered, the cross planted on heathen shores. But of more tangible results there were few. One court official seemed to sum up the general verdict on the discovery of the Solomons when he wrote:

In my opinion, according to the report I have received, they were of little importance, although they said that they heard of better lands; for in the course of these discoveries they found no specimens of spices, nor of gold and silver, nor of any other source of profit, and all the people were naked savages.

Twenty years later Mendana, older and wearier but still willing to believe the best of everyone, made another voyage in search of the Solomons, but missed the main group of islands altogether. Instead he landed on Ndeni in the Santa Cruz group and there tried to establish a colony. It was a dismal failure: the natives were hostile, the physical conditions worse, and many Spaniards died, Mendana among them. The rest sailed miserably back to Peru. The Solomons were not to be disturbed again by Europeans for 200 years.

By the end of the sixteenth century a number of explorers had crossed the Pacific. With the exception of Magellan and Mendana and their expeditions the Church had made little impression on the people of the islands. Most ships carried their men of God but not all of them were as spiritual and intelligent as Mendana's Father Francisco. Some were at loggerheads with their captains; one of these was the priest who accompanied Francis Drake on his voyage round the world. After a particularly vitriolic altercation Drake organised a special ceremony and "excommunicated" his turbulent priest. It may have been in fun, but everyone got the message and the priest was less troublesome for the remainder of the circumnavigation.

Then came a man who was to personify the spiritual crusading attitude of the earlier conquistadors. This was Pedro Fernandez de Quiros, the last of the great explorers to sail from Peru, and another Portuguese to offer his services to Spain. With the dawn of the seventeenth century the great age of Spanish exploration was coming to an end and the exploits of Quiros stand out all the more clearly against the background of general lassitude.

He seems to have been a very pleasant man, which is one of the more unlikely adjectives to apply to a trail-blazer of his time. He was certainly extremely competent at his profession. He had accompanied Mendana on that unfortunate captain's last expedition and was responsible for bringing the survivors safely back to the American continent. Before his death Mendana described his chief pilot as "an officer of known worth, experienced in all the perils of the sea, and learned in many things of the heaven".

Quiros was also extremely devout, more so even than Mendana. The latter had accepted implicitly the tenets of his faith and always adhered to them, but Quiros went further. His fervour was of the evangelical sort, and on his return from Mendana's fatal voyage spent much of his time planning to return to the islands where there were so many souls to be saved.

Unhappily on the reverse side of the coin Quiros possessed a number of shortcomings — he was disorganised; he was not a disciplinarian; he tended towards naivety; worst of all, he was accident-prone. Things tended to happen to Quiros.

But always he was enthusiastic. He wanted to lead an expedition back to the Pacific to go on where Mendana had been forced to leave off. He approached the local authorities in Mexico: please could he have money to fit out several ships? The administrators would have none of him — Quiros would have to approach the

King in Spain — at his own expense. Undaunted, he took passage to Spain, but his lack of good fortune caught up with him almost at once, for the fleet in which he was sailing ran into a storm and a number of ships sank. The rest put into harbour and stayed there almost a year while an English force blockaded the entrance.

Finally the navigator reached Europe, only to find that it was Holy Year. Quiros was not a man to ignore the niceties of conduct. Selling everything that he possessed, he purchased a robe and a staff and set out to walk to Rome. He got there; what is more, he secured an audience with the Pope and received the latter's blessing for the proposed expedition. Things were looking up. Quiros went to Spain and asked King Philip for royal permission.

The red tape at court almost choked him, but he persevered. "I was forced to be more importunate to his Majesty, submitting new memorials every day." Eventually the King assented and a jubilant Quiros headed back for America.

He ran into more trouble in the Atlantic. At Guadeloupe more than fifty members of the ship's crew were killed by the islanders; the frigate in which Quiros was travelling smashed itself against some rocks. Quiros and the others constructed a new vessel out of the wreckage and sailed to fetch help for the crews of other craft shipwrecked at the same time. Their makeshift vessel reached the mainland and took help back to the castaways.

Quiros then returned to his business, but no-one wanted to know about his royal order. He reached Panama where a religious procession was taking place and Quiros went out on to a balcony to watch. The balcony collapsed, killing a priest and putting Quiros in hospital for ten weeks. When he came out he had no money with which to pay his bills. Without food or provisions he staggered on to Peru, begging for shelter en route. Again his story was greeted with indifference, again this indomitable man persisted. Eventually he secured an audience with the Viceroy and got his sanction: by the end of the year he had been given three small ships, a tiny fleet assembled and provisioned at a total cost of 184,000 ducats. Among the 300 men on board were six Franciscan friars and four nursing brothers of the order of John of God. The second in command was the capable and determined Luis Vaez de Torres, later to discover and name the strait north of Australia; the pilot, who was to cause Quiros a great deal of trouble, was a mercurial man called Juan Bilboa.

At last, thirty months after leaving Spain with the royal permission for his journey, Quiros was almost ready to depart. His frustrations were not yet over, however. It had been his intention to mark the imminent departure of his fleet with a procession in sackcloth through the streets, but the authorities forbade it. As Quiros himself darkly put it, "the envy which is so powerful put an end to this laudable intention". Nevertheless the send-off was enthusiastic enough even for Quiros's drama-loving soul, for huge crowds watched the three ships glide out of the harbour on 21 December 1605. The Franciscans chanted the *Te Deum* and Quiros ordered guns to be fired. Hardly had the coast passed out of sight behind him than Quiros, ingenuous as ever, decreed that the Pacific Ocean would from then on be known as the "Gulf of Our Lady of Loretto" in honour of the patron saint of the expedition.

Quarrelling broke out within the month, as soon, in fact, as the ships struck bad weather. Quiros had been ill but soon regained his feet "for whom God wishes will live". The crew became apprehensive as Quiros continued to plough onwards west-south-west, and Torres and Bilboa were involved in almost daily bickering. Quiros, obsessed with his dreams of discovery, could not maintain order. By 22 January he allowed himself to be persuaded to change his course to west-north-west, to the great chagrin of Torres. Had they continued on their original route it appears likely that they would have discovered New Zealand. Quiros was disappointed but not heartbroken at the change of direction. The expedition was in the Lord's hands; He would bring them to land. In the meantime there were daily prayers, a strict ban on cursing, dice and cards. Anyone heard blaspheming would lose a day's ration of food. This was a considerable deprivation because by the standards of the time the allocation of provisions to each man was generous — $1\frac{1}{2}$ lb biscuit, 1 lb meat, 2 oz bacon and a half gallon of drinking water.

Quiros also laid down careful plans for the treatment of any natives encountered when they struck land: no native was to be abused nor was his property to be taken; a paternal note if possible was to be struck, but at first all islanders were to be treated with caution in case they should prove warlike; it must be remembered at all times that members of the expedition were representatives of Christendom, the first the natives would have met.

The ships sailed on; of how many early voyages that could be said! Supplies of water dwindled, malcontents among the sailors grew bolder. Quiros insisted that there would be a landfall; there was, he assured his men, either a chain of islands or a whole new continent stretching from the Straits of Magellan to New Guinea. At the very least there was Santa Cruz somewhere ahead of them; had he not been there with Mendana? It was only a matter of persevering long enough for them to sight land. Bilboa, the chief pilot, refuted such airy notions. On 25 March he announced triumphantly that they had sailed 2,220 leagues, and as Quiros had claimed that Santa Cruz lay only 1,850 leagues from Peru it was obvious that their leader was either lying or mistaken, devious or incompetent. Quiros called a meeting at which he selfrighteously denounced Bilboa, asserting that he had discovered an error of 600 leagues in the pilot's reckoning. So it went on, accusation and defence, claim and counterclaim under the blazing sun.

Eventually they encountered a few scattered atolls and islands, some of them inhabited, but still no water, or at least not in sufficient quantity for their needs, only coconut milk. They landed at one of the Cook Islands. Quiros gave the customary instructions for a number of hostages to be seized and held until water was forthcoming from the other islanders. The natives objected to this cavalier treatment and offered resistance, an odd way to greet the bringers of Christianity. Naturally they had to be taught a lesson; there was a short sharp encounter and the islanders fled inland, leaving their dead on the beach.

On 7 April they sighted Taumako in the Duff Islands, only a few days' sail, though Quiros did not know it, from Santa Cruz. At first the islanders contemplated resistance but the discharge of a Spanish musket put an end to such inhospitable thoughts and the chief came out in suitably humble and ingratiating manner to welcome the visitors. The friars went ashore and said Mass. Their actions were imitated earnestly by the local inhabitants; Mendana, too, had noticed the ability of the islanders to imitate European gestures and habits almost at first sight. If only he had time, sighed Quiros, it would probably be just as easy to inculcate the deeper meaning of Christianity into such people. He could not stay for much more than a week, however. Taumako was plainly an isolated island, and he was looking for a continent.

On 18 April the Spaniards left. They ran into a little rough weather and when it cleared Quiros was asked what course should be set. The expedition now had water and confidence. The leader answered, "Put the ships' heads where they like, for God will guide them as may be right." In the event they went south-west and soon found themselves sailing among a number of lovely islands. They landed at one of them, Gaua in the Banks Islands, and a member of the crew attempted to reassure the inhabitants by telling them: "We come from the east, we are Christians, we seek you and we want you to be ours." To be on the safe side the Spaniards took several hostages but released them, with gifts, on receipt of food and water from the other islanders.

Not even these attractive islands, Quiros decided with real regret, could be regarded as the long-sought-for continent. At the end of April, however, to his almost unbounded joy and satisfaction, he discovered what he took to be the great unknown land mass. The Spaniards sailed into a deep and handsome bay situated against a backdrop of impressive mountains falling away into the distance. Expeditions ashore marvelled at the fruits and abundant vegetation to be found there. There was a large expanse of flat land, suitable for the site of a town, many trees for the buildings, fresh water and a great deal of wild life to be hunted for food.

With pride and gratitude Quiros named his discovery Terra Austrialia del Espiritu Santo. The "Austrialia" was in honour of Philip III of Spain who was also Archduke of Austria. The rest of the title was bestowed because as far as the leader of the expedition was concerned this really was the farthest land of the holy spirit.

In fact it was one of the islands of the New Hebrides group. Quiros continued to regard the area as a fragment of the expected continent, which accounts for the grandiose and rather pretentious actions that were to follow the discovery, actions that seem absurd, when considered in the harsh light of reality, as taking place on a remote tropical island. Had they occurred on a continent the size of North America, for example, as Quiros believed, then they would have appeared a little less fantastic, though still bizarre enough.

In the first place, in order to guard against possible attacks from the inhabitants, who had showed resentment at having their home invaded, the leader of the expedition drew up an elaborate chain of command in which his subordinates received titles rather more impressive than the circumstances would seem to warrant. Torres was made camp master, which was only according to custom, but the setting up of a Ministry of War and Marine does seem a trifle over-ornate. The plans for the proposed settlement of New Jerusalem were also somewhat ambitious. The crowning irony occurred when Quiros announced the establishment of a new order, the Knights of the Holy Ghost, "with the constitutions and precepts to be kept and professed, guided by such lofty and Christian ends as will be seen in them when the Lord is served, as I shall be able to show".

Though perhaps lacking in a sense of proportion and apt to make himself appear ridiculous even in the eyes of his contemporaries, Quiros lacked nothing in piety and devotion. At his instructions the friars constructed an altar and at a ceremony on the beach the first church in the New Hebrides was dedicated. Called "Our Lady of Loretto", it was consecrated in front of three companies of men drawn up with banners held high. Quiros knelt in the sand and said a prayer and then after a procession the friars raised the orangewood cross. Quiros said a few words and his secretary and companion, Bermudez the poet, read a poem especially composed for the occasion. The opening lines went:

> Behold how we have found these lands,
> Now clearly seen by mortal ken,
> These are regions now made known,
> Pressed by feet of Christian men.

Quiros then took possession of the islands "in the name of the most Holy Trinity" and the leading friar led the company in prayers, asking that the natives of the land be turned to the knowledge of the true Lord. The assembled Europeans cried "Long live the King of Spain", three banners were unfurled, four

Masses said, two slaves liberated, all the guns fired and some food was stolen from the local inhabitants.

Alas, Nouva Jerusalema lasted only thirty-five days. Even though Quiros had selected magistrates and a chief constable and sworn them into office the realisation slowly dawned that the whole affair was too impracticable. The natives were implacably hostile and there was a series of bloody clashes between the Spaniards and the islanders. Quiros's subordinates were divided as to whether they should stay or leave; certainly none of them shared their leader's belief in the golden city he had hoped to establish. Perhaps Quiros was convinced by their arguments, perhaps he grew weary of the whole matter, perhaps by now he appreciated that he was no administrator. Early in June they left the island of Vera Cruz and headed back towards Peru.

But their adventures had not ended; the three ships became separated, whether by accident or design has never been established. Quiros eventually reached Acapulco and was given passage to Europe. He never went exploring again. Distrusted by the authorities, he spent the rest of his life trying to gain backing for another expedition. Nothing went right for him. He pawned the royal banner that had flown over his discoveries, wrote many letters and received no satisfactory answers. In 1614, disappointed, impoverished and neglected, he died. Quiros had not been given the opportunity of taking the word of God once more across the Pacific.

Three hundred years after Magellan — a Roman Catholic chapel at Bacor, Philippines. From *Résumé de l'Histoire de l'Océanie*, by M. M. C. Henricy et de Rienzi, Librarie Historique et d'éducation, Bruxelles, 1847.

2

WHO WILL MINISTER TO THE HEATHEN?

After the Spanish came the Dutch, doggedly inching their way across the Pacific by way of the Cape of Good Hope or occasionally, to the fury of the Spaniards, via Cape Horn in their search for gold and trade. In the same year that Quiros attempted to establish New Jerusalem the Dutchman Jansz sailed along the coast of New Guinea and later saw the shoreline of Australia. In 1616 Hartog was discovering new islands and by the middle years of the century such seamen as Van Noort, Spielberg, Schouten, and Le Maire had all ventured into the Pacific. Some of them had even prowled along the northern coast of Australia, though opinion was divided as to whether the land mass was a continent or a series of islands. In 1642 Abel Tasman did much to resolve this controversy by sailing, albeit at a respectful distance, right round New Holland, as it was known. He also named Van Dieman's Land (Tasmania), saw and named New Zealand, and sailed past some of the islands of Fiji and Tonga.

Where the Dutch went it was a reasonable certainty that Great Britain, the other major European seafaring nation, would follow. The first swarm of British seamen to descend like hornets on the Pacific — men of the calibre of Dampier, Cowley, Cavendish and Woods-Rogers — were prompted by no idealistic motives. Most of them were buccaneers. For a relatively brief period the Pacific was to prove a lucrative if dangerous hunting ground for them. They harried the Spanish settlements on the west coast of America and did their best to intercept the treasure ships sailing between Mexico and Manila. The quest for prizes sometimes resulted in magnificent voyages of exploration — Dampier in 1688 was the first Englishman to visit New Holland, an exploit he repeated in 1700 — but such discoveries were merely incidental to the main theme.

Slowly the details of the fabulous islands of the Pacific began to penetrate to the cities of Europe and America, though it was not until the end of the eighteenth century that the image of the islands as a trouble-free paradise seems to have been established. Most expeditions had far more prosaic intentions than a desire to reach an idyllic never-never land. Certainly such voyages as those undertaken by Roggeveen when he discovered Easter Island in 1722, and the marvellous circumnavigation of the world by Anson twenty years later, struck a chord in the romantic imaginations of those who stayed at home, but by the later years of the eighteenth century most expeditions to the Pacific were either for the advancement of science or the promotion of commerce. Britons like Byron, Carteret and Wallis all captained voyages across the Pacific in the 1760s, and they were followed by such Frenchmen as Bougainville, Marion and La Pérouse.

It was Captain James Cook, however, who really aroused the interest of his fellow-countrymen in the South Sea with his three voyages to the Pacific between 1768 and 1779 when he was killed at Hawaii. Cook's voyages of exploration caught the imagination of the public to an extent never before equalled. Starting with his initial journey to allow scientists to witness the transit of the planet Venus across the sun, a rare event and one from which such calculations as the distance of the earth from the sun could be made, Cook achieved a tremendous reputation as a Pacific navigator and explorer. Among his instructions from the Admiralty for his first expedition Cook had been directed "to observe with accuracy the situation of such islands as you may discover in the course of your voyage that have not hitherto been discovered by any Europeans, and take possession for His Majesty". His superiors must have been well satisfied with the manner in which Cook complied with his orders, for in the course of his three voyages he had visited Australia and New Zealand, charted many Polynesian islands and even probed Antarctica.

His published journals were bestsellers. Cook was not alone among the Pacific seafarers in this respect, for almost everybody who managed to reach the South Sea seemed to write about it. In Britain, starting with the eccentric Alexander Dalrymple and his *An Account of the Discoveries Made in the South Pacific Ocean Previous to 1764,* such luminaries as Byron, Carteret, and Joseph Banks all published accounts of what they had seen and heard on the far side of the world, and so did many of the

A human sacrifice, in "Otaheite". An engraving after John Webber, RA, in *A voyage to the Pacific Ocean . . .* published in 1784, the official account of Cook's third voyage.

lesser lights who had accompanied them. These tales of handsome brown-skinned men and beautiful dusky maidens living lives of ease under the tropic sun gave rise to a Pacific vogue and by 1800 books and plays with a South Seas background were extremely popular.

Not that Britain had a monopoly in the Pacific. The French were there in some force and were to become particularly strong in New Caledonia, the Loyalty Islands, Tahiti and the Marquesas. Spain still possessed the Philippines and the Carolines, and Russian fur traders were working in the Aleutians. The First Fleet carrying its convicts had arrived at Botany Bay on 26 January 1788. The Pacific and its islands were known by repute in most areas of the world. The islands as a source of revenue also entered into the scheme of things. Whalers were the first to sail the Pacific in search of their prey; some of them took on board men from the islands, who returned to their homes with stories of other parts of the ocean they had visited. It was a two-way traffic; some seamen on whalers deserted at the more attractive islands and lived with the local people, the first European beachcombers.

Later, escaped convicts from the island penal settlements and Australia also reached some of the South Sea islands. After the whalers came the sandalwood dealers and then the collectors of pearl shell and *bêche de mer,* the sea slug considered a delicacy by the Chinese.

By the closing years of the eighteenth century adventurers and traders were flocking to the Pacific. Most of them headed for Australia in the first instance and then used the continent as a springboard for ventures into the Pacific. Some of them, especially the sandalwood traders, were to bring bloodshed and disaster to the islands in the early years of the nineteenth century. It became increasingly obvious that there was no effective means of enforcing the law in this remote part of the world; the islands were open for exploitation.

The many problems facing the inhabitants of the Pacific Islands were acknowledged by thinking people in Britain and other Western countries. The Christian nations of the world felt a responsibility towards the islanders, and in Britain in particular the Churches were becoming increasingly aware of their obligations. *Go ye into all the world and preach the gospel to every creature,* Christ had told his followers and it was an edict taken very much to heart by the devout in eighteenth-century Britain. The Society for the Propagation of the Gospel in Foreign Parts had been formed as early as 1701, and missionaries had been going forth to the colonies throughout the century, the missions to India arousing particular interest at home. In 1786, before the death of John Wesley, their founder, the Methodists under Dr Coke had been going overseas, and similar work was to be encouraged by Wilberforce and others on behalf of the Anglicans. In 1792 the Baptist Missionary Society had been formed and three years later came the birth of the London Missionary Society. In answer to the question, "Who will minister to the heathen?", a surprisingly large number of people responded.

The London Missionary Society was the first to send missionaries from Britain to the Pacific. Founded by a number of ministers and laymen of various Protestant denominations on Friday, 25 September 1795 for the purpose of sending the word of the Lord to "Otaheite [Tahiti], or some other of the islands of the South Sea", it owed much to the enthusiasm of two men,

Joseph Hardcastle, a London merchant and treasurer of the society, and the Rev. Dr Haweis.

Haweis had been interested in the South Sea islands almost as soon as he had heard about them. He had been much taken with the exploits of Captain Bligh, the doughty early navigator of the Pacific whose skill as a seaman seems to have been equalled only by his irascibility and lack of judgment of men. Bligh it was who, shortly before becoming involved in the famous mutiny had sent the ill-timed message: "We are all in good spirits and my little ship fit to go round half a score of worlds. My men are all active good fellows, and what has given me much pleasure is that I have not yet been obliged to punish any one. My officers and young gentlemen are all tractable and well-disposed, and we now understand each other so well that we shall remain so the whole voyage: . . ." These were words that might well have returned to haunt Bligh as he steered his cutter on its epic voyage after he had been deposed as captain of the *Bounty*.

Nevertheless, Haweis shared the general admiration of Bligh as a navigator, and even tried to send two missionaries to the Pacific on Bligh's second voyage to the South Seas. He succeeded in attracting the interest of the Countess of Huntingdon and obtaining

Idols "worshipped by the inhabitants of the South Sea Islands". From *Polynesian Researches, Volume II*, by William Ellis, Fisher, Son, & Jackson, London, 1829.

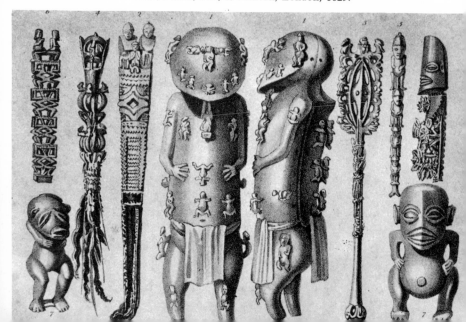

the permission of the Government and was able to offer "£500 for the equipment of the first Missionary that should be sent on this blessed service". Two men offered themselves but because they were not graduates could not be ordained and both volunteers lost interest in the matter.

Haweis, however, was made of sterner stuff and did not relax his efforts to send a mission to Tahiti. In 1796 he had his way. Backed by the London Missionary Society a ship and crew were procured to take a group to Tahiti. There were thirty-nine people in the party of missionaries, six of whom were wives, and three children. Only four of the men were ordained ministers, the rest were lay-preachers. It was very much a lower middle class party, and the laymen were for the most part tradesmen. A contemporary list shows the trades followed by some of the missionaries:

Mr Shelley	Cabinetmaker	Mr Buchanan	Tailor
Mr Kelso	Weaver	Mr Cooper	Shoemaker
Mr Wilkinson	Carpenter	Mr Nobbs	Hatter
Mr Bowell	Shopkeeper	Mr Veeson	Bricklayer

Among other trades represented were those of butcher, cooper, cotton operative, harnessmaker, gardener, gentleman's servant, and a number of others. Much has been made of the lack of suitability of such artisans as missionaries to the Pacific. A great deal has been written to show that people of such limited education and puritanical leanings should have been the last to be allowed to minister to the free-and-easy islanders. It is true that some of the missionaries were completely out of their depth in the carefree environment of the South Seas, but it is only too easy to poke fun at their mistakes and misunderstandings. Not enough has been made of their courage and piety, their simple faith and determination. To leave England for the unknown islands took more than the ordinary amount of devotion, especially for a bunch of artisans who had hardly travelled from their own back yards. Perseverance and character in plenty were to be found among these men and women.

They left London early on the morning of 10 August 1796. The official history of the LMS tells us that "the Missionaries embarked at Blackwall, multitudes flocking around them to take their leave;

and as they sailed down the river, singing the praises of God, the scene became still more deeply affecting". They reached Spithead and were there detained for some time. Finally all was ready and Haweis went on board to say his farewells, later writing of the scene in the *Evangelical Magazine*: "We believed we should meet and pray no more together, but we vowed to remember each other before the Throne daily, and knew we should shortly unite in that kingdom, where our prayers should be exchanged for everlasting praises."

The ship they sailed in was the *Duff*. It flew the missionary flag, three doves with olive branches in their beaks shown against a purple background, and was captained by James Wilson, himself a Christian and a man who had for a time been a prisoner of Hyder Ali in India. Among the instructions given him by the London Missionary Society was one for settling his passengers when they reached the islands: "When you consider the qualifications of the Missionaries you will perhaps be inclined to think that remaining in one or two bodies they may form models of civilized society, small indeed, but tolerably complete."

The voyage was long — it was seven months before they reached Tahiti — and not without incident. There was a certain amount of seasickness and a great deal of praying and hymn-singing. Many of the missionaries kept diaries — this first expedition of the London Missionary Society was certainly well documented. The man who seems to have created the most favourable impression was Samuel Gaulton, something of an unknown factor, who joined at the last minute but who conducted himself with such propriety and willingness that he was unanimously elected a member of the mission and designated a place on the expedition to the Friendly Islands, should the *Duff* ever get there.

Even to the more optimistic among the missionaries it must sometimes have been a matter for conjecture whether they would ever reach their destination. It took them a considerable time to reach Rio de Janeiro and even then they had 14,000 more miles to go. This was caused by a decision not to risk the Cape Horn passage but to sail back across the Atlantic and make for the South Sea by way of the Cape of Good Hope.

Eventually they succeeded. After passing south of Australia and New Zealand the *Duff* reached Tahiti on Saturday, 4 March

The London Missionary Society's vessel *Duff* arriving at "Otaheite". An oil print by Kronheim and Co. in the Alexander Turnbull Library, Wellington.

1797, though it was not until the following day that the missionaries were ready to go ashore. The Tahitians who came out to the ship greeted the Europeans affably. The islanders were a charming, beautiful and indolent people who had already received sporadic visits from white men. Wallis had landed there in 1767 and so had Bougainville. The Frenchman had been particularly impressed with the warmth of his reception and the beauty of the women:

The canoes were filled with women, who in the charm of their features conceded nothing to most European females, and who in beauty of form could easily rival them all. Most of these nymphs were naked, for the men and old women who were with them had taken off the loin-cloths which they usually wore . . . I ask you — how in the midst of such a spectacle could one keep at work four hundred Frenchmen, young sailors, and who had not seen any women for six months?

Two years later Captain Cook had also landed at the island, and while not unappreciative of the charms of its women had found time to make a note of the layout of the land:

Between the foot of the ridges and the sea is a border of low land surrounding the whole island, except in a few places where the ridges rise directly from the sea, this low land is of various breadths but nowhere exceeds a mile and a half; the soil is rich and fertile being for the most part well stocked with fruit trees and small plantations and well watered by a number of small rivulets of excellent water which comes from the adjacent hills. It is upon this low land that the greatest part of the inhabitants live, not in towns and villages but dispersed everywhere around the whole island.

The *Duff* missionaries were not the first to attempt to establish a church on the island, for as early as 1772 two Franciscans had been landed at Tahiti by a Spanish vessel from Peru. The two Spaniards had set up a cross but could make no impression on the islanders, who scoffed at them. The Franciscans persevered for three years but were eventually taken off by another Spanish ship and returned to Lima.

The British missionaries were undeterred by such a precedent. On 5 March, the Sabbath, the Rev. Mr Cover conducted a service for them all, watched attentively by a number of Tahitians. He took as his text "God is love" from the first epistle of John, and though the islanders made little of the sermon they seemed to approve of the hymn-singing. Among those who greeted Captain Wilson and his band was the High Priest of Oro. Later the heir to the throne, who was to become Pomare II, arrived. He was about seventeen at this time and did not seem impressed with what he saw; but his father, Pomare I, was more hospitable. He assured the missionaries that they would be free to live in the area around Matavai Bay, where the *Duff* had dropped anchor. This led to the first of many misunderstandings, for the missionaries thought they had been given the land. The king, however, had had no such intention — no foreigner was allowed the unrestricted ownership of land on Tahiti, and this was not realised by the Englishmen for some time. In the meantime they prevailed on the islanders

The high priest of Tahiti ceding the district of Matavai to Captain Wilson for the missionaries. Engraving by H. Robinson, painted by R. Smirke, RA. A plate in *Polynesian Researches, Vol I*, by William Ellis, London, 1829.

to build a settlement for them, which was done willingly enough, and when it was completed an impressive ceremony was held to mark the occasion, with the missionaries dressed in frock coats.

When Captain Wilson had satisfied himself that all seemed to be settling in well on Tahiti he left to perform the second part of his task, which was to land ten missionaries at Tonga. Captain Cook had reported so favourably on the friendship encountered on this island — "They showed every kind of attention and civility" — that the London Missionary Society had marked it down as a suitable place for their preachers.

They landed at Tonga on 12 April after being welcomed by a number of chiefs, but the island was not as friendly as the missionaries had hoped. The previous night while at anchor the *Duff* had been surrounded by a large number of canoes and during a storm the natives tried to cut the ship's cable which would probably have resulted in the vessel being wrecked on a reef, but the seamen drove the islanders away by hurling coconuts at them. The chiefs, however, promised the missionaries their protection, and rather nervously the Europeans ventured ashore. One of the leaders seemed to be a man called Ulukalala, the brother of a Tongan who had befriended Captain Cook. The missionaries were somewhat afraid of this man — one of them described him in his journal as being "about forty years of age, of a sullen, morose countenance; speaks very little, but when angry, bellows forth with a voice like the roaring of a lion".

Wilson cannot have been as easy about leaving the missionaries on Tonga as he had been at sailing away from Tahiti, but there was one more port of call to be made and on 14 April the *Duff* left for the Marquesas. These too had been visited earlier by Cook, and though he had encountered some trouble it was decided by the LMS to send two missionaries there. Perhaps the words of Quiros when he had stopped at the islands almost two hundred years before influenced the missionaries: after seeing one particularly handsome young man, Quiros wrote: "Never in my life have I felt such a pain as I do now, to think that such a fair creature might be left to go to perdition."

At any rate Brothers Crook and Harris were selected to establish a mission in the Marquesas. Crook proved to be a man of considerable courage and initiative, but Harris had an unhappy

time. As soon as the *Duff* anchored off Ohitahoo it was greeted by
two attractive women who swam out from the island and circled
the ship calling out *"Waheine! Waheine!"* ("We are women!").
The circumspect Wilson refused to allow them on board, perhaps
mindful of Bougainville's earlier remarks on seeing the beautiful
Tahitian women approaching his ship.

Crook and Harris were sent ashore, and the following morning
a ship's boat cautiously made its way from the *Duff* to the beach.
The crew saw one of the missionaries sitting forlornly on the chest
containing his belongings at the water's edge: it was Harris and
he had quite a story to tell. It appeared that he and Crook had
been greeted in a friendly manner by a local chief who had taken
them to his village. After a while the chief had offered to take
them inland to another village. Crook had been eager to go but
Harris had refused, whereupon the chief had gone off with Crook,
telling his wife to look after the remaining missionary. Unfortunately for Harris the chief's wife had put an over-generous inter-
pretation on her husband's parting remark, and the scandalised
missionary finally had to reject the woman's overtures. She had
gone off in a huff, leaving Harris to sleep on the floor. But
brooding on his brusque dismissal the woman had begun to
entertain doubts as to his sex, and accompanied by other women
of the village she had swooped on the sleeping man and conducted
a practical examination in order to clear up the matter. Harris had
torn himself free and fled for the beach where the sailors had
found him. He absolutely refused to remain on the island, but
Crook, the former gentleman's servant, chose to remain and the
Duff left him at the Marquesas.

This meant that by the summer of 1797 the London Missionary
Society had representatives on three Pacific Islands — Tahiti,
Tonga, and the Marquesas. The main mission was at Tahiti while
the other two were regarded as outposts. Tahiti managed to keep
going as a mission station but the others were not long in coming
to grief. In the Marquesas Crook did his courageous best, beset
by mischievous islanders and occasional European beachcombers,
to teach the natives better methods of farming, even taking
turnip seeds with him on his forays, but from the beginning
he was fighting a losing battle. In 1797 he returned sadly
to London, but his days as a missionary were not ended for

later he sailed once more to Tahiti where he did good work.

The missionaries left on Tonga also had a difficult time. On 16 April, two days after the *Duff* had sailed, they celebrated their first Sabbath with Brother Buchanan preaching from Jeremiah, chapter 32, verse 27: "Behold, I am the Lord, the God of all flesh; is there anything too hard for me?" It was, under the circumstances, a courageous text.

At first the Europeans stayed together, but later they separated, each group coming under the protection of a different chief. They persevered but when the *Duff* returned later in the year one of the missionaries had had enough and sailed away on her. The Europeans were given land by their hosts but it soon became apparent that it was the iron tools possessed by the missionaries that the Tongans wanted, not the word of God. Some of the tools were stolen and altogether they had an unhappy time. Their condition was not improved when it was found that there were two Europeans already on the island, deserters from a sailing ship. One of them, a Londoner named Ambler, knew the language and condescended to act as interpreter for the missionaries, but his companion, Connelly, a glib rogue from Cork, made it plain from the beginning that he had no time for them.

The deserters did not at first trouble them, though later they were to be a thorn in their flesh, especially when joined by a third beachcomber, variously named Morgan and Morgan Bryan in contemporary accounts. It was the islanders who grew tired of their devout visitors, wearying even of the cuckoo clock owned by the missionaries, which was called *akaulea* or "talking wood" by the Tongans. They were willing to tolerate Europeans who conformed to their own standards of (to European eyes) libidinous and pugnacious behaviour, as witness their hospitality to a motley host of deserters and escaped convicts over the years, but the sober and rather inward-looking Christians puzzled and eventually repelled them.

They did, however, give a joyous welcome to one sheep who deserted the missionary fold. This was Veeson who had been living with the chief Mulikiha'amea. He abandoned his fellows and took to the life of a country gentleman with considerable aplomb. The chief gave him fifteen acres of land with many coconut and plantain trees and dotted with the dwellings of thirty natives who became George Veeson's servants. The renegade grew yams, *kava* roots, *taro* and fruit on his estate and took to himself a steady supply of native "wives", whom he was apt to change at short notice. One of nature's survivors, Veeson lived through the subsequent civil war on the island, returned to England and engaged in a rather spectacular transformation in which he repented publicly of his sins and wrote, with the aid of a literary "ghost", a bestselling book about his experiences in the Pacific. It was a tome unctuous in style and extremely respectful to authority in general and the London Missionary Society in particular. Of his fellow missionaries Veeson wrote ingratiatingly:

Considering all the obstacles, it must be a great satisfaction to the promoters of the South Sea Mission, to be assured from one who has to condemn himself, and who remained at Tongataboo (Tonga) after all the brethren left it, that no other of the Missionaries whom he accompanied thither, acted unbecoming their sacred character.

At the time the remaining eight missionaries could have done with more concrete support from their departed brother than this delayed unsolicited and unwanted testimonial, but they were not going to get it. Veeson was lost, temporarily at least, to the devil. Soon the missionaries had more pressing problems with which to contend and their former companion was all but forgotten. Even after the Christians had been on Tonga for some months they still had made little contact with the people. There was the almost insurmountable language barrier — their interpreter, Connelly, might be prevailed upon to translate urgent messages; he was certainly not going to deliver sermons for them!

Anyway, the Tongans had enough gods of their own to be in need of imported ones. There were the Tagaloas in the sky, the Mauis in the underworld, and Hikule'o who presided over the Tongan paradise of Bulotu. Only chiefs possessed souls and these went in due course to Bulotu. The spirits of the dead could cause a great deal of trouble, and as no Tongan would want to offend against them, a series of taboos was in operation to prevent such transgressions. Most gods were all-powerful; there were gods of the wind, the sea, the harvest, and each god had his priest or earthly representative to whom tribute had to be paid.

Against such a well-developed and all-embracing system the

missionaries, unable to speak the language and lacking the cheerful extrovert personalities beloved of the Tongans, could do little. Their services, held behind closed doors in order to prevent the islanders scoffing, began to worry the Tongans. Matters were not helped when some of the beachcombers, seeing in the missionaries forbidding signs of the coming of law and order, began to spread stories about them. They told the credulous islanders that the reason for the hymns and prayers of the Christians was to bring down a mighty plague on the islands of Tonga. The missionaries had been sent, declared the beachcombers, to take over the island on behalf of the King of England and in order to render the Tongans powerless they were first to be decimated by disease.

The islanders were probably ready to believe any evil of the lacklustre visitors, but when the spate of rumours was followed by an actual epidemic which killed a number of people, including the king, Mumi, suspicion hardened to certainty. Mumi died in the same year that the missionaries landed, and at his funeral the missionaries made themselves even more unpopular by their obvious revulsion at the sight of some of the death customs of the people, a number of which had been introduced from Fiji. Two widows of the king were strangled at his grave, and at the customary feasting which lasted for weeks many men cut themselves with knives and spears as a sign of their sorrow.

Somehow the Christians managed to struggle on, despised and ignored by the Tongans on most occasions, treated with the utmost suspicion at others. Things came to a head two years later, in 1799, when civil war broke out; it started when Finau Ukalala, one of the chiefs who had met the *Duff* on its first arrival, assassinated the tyrant Tuku'aho who had succeeded Mumi. For a period there was great confusion among the other chiefs, some supporting the cause of the dead Tuku'aho while others threw in their lot with the rebels under Finau Ukalala. The unfortunate missionaries were scattered among both sides. Veeson, who certainly seemed to have been a brave man, joined in the fighting with a will, supporting his patron on the side of the rebels. His first battle was successful, and the renegade wrote with some relish of the aftermath: "After our engagement, our victorious troops took the bodies of their slain enemies, dragged them to the sea-shore, and after inflicting every brutal insult of savage cruelty, roasted and ate them. . . ."

The missionaries of course took no sides, but their neutrality was not accepted by the Tongans. Three of them, Bowell, Harper, and Gaulton, found themselves in the path of a retreat. Gaulton was the missionary who had joined the expedition in Britain at the last moment and who had so impressed the others on the trip out to Tahiti. Some of the fleeing Tongans tried to persuade the Europeans to go with them, but Gaulton and his companions refused. When the advancing army entered the village which now contained only the missionaries and a sailor who had joined them, they were clubbed to death by a Tongan who had once been refused an axe by the Europeans.

The bodies were left for weeks in the open until discovered by the surviving Christians. One of them described the scene: "We found brothers Bowell and Gaulton upon the road, very near to each other; brother Harper lay in the adjoining field about fifty yards nearer home; they were all so much disfigured that we could not have known any of them but for the natives who had often seen them since their death."

It was virtually the end of the first expedition to the Friendly Islands. The remaining missionaries escaped with their lives but were forced to hide in caves and keep on the move until the war finally ended. When in 1800 a sailing vessel called at Tonga the five surviving missionaries boarded it. During their three years among the islands one of their number had left before a year was up, another had left the mission and three had been murdered. Not one Tongan had been converted to Christianity.

That left Tahiti, and the situation was not much better there, not in the early years at least. According to their stated aim the missionaries tried to set up some sort of routine so that the islanders could see the Christian tenets being practised as a normal part of everyday life. One of the Europeans gave an account of those early days:

We drew up rules for every day's work, the bell to ring at six; to be assembled for prayer in half an hour; to labour till ten at our various occupations; to spend from ten to three in mental improvements; from three till night at our usual employment; bell to ring at seven for prayer, and the journal to be

The Rev. Henry Nott. A wood engraving from *The story of the South Seas,* by George Cousins 1894.

read. We then proceeded to divide our iron for traffic, and cast lots for the watches.

Almost immediately the Europeans, every one a trader or craftsman steeped in the profit motive, ran foul of the aimiable Tahitian custom of helping oneself to anything that took one's fancy. The islanders did not want to *buy* goods that could be taken by sleight of hand. The missionaries, with some lack of logic, were prepared to accept land and labour from the islanders but raised a great fuss when the Tahitians in turn helped themselves to nails or tools that happened to attract them. One islander went so far as to steal the clothes of Brother Gillham as he swam in a river, and the enraged missionaries apprehended the culprit and chained him to a pillar. In order to discourage such thefts Brother Nott, a man who was rapidly coming to the forefront of the missionaries on Tahiti and who was the first to attempt to learn the language, preached a fiery sermon on the subject of theft. His words seem to have gone home because several stolen items were returned.

Disenchantment set in on both sides. The Tahitians, encouraged to abandon their songs and music, to force themselves into the European clothes provided by the missionaries, and to observe the Sabbath as a day devoid of light entertainment, began to wonder just what sort of men they had encouraged to join them. Some of them, overawed, began to comply with the requests, or demands, that they become members of a sober and God-fearing community. The beautiful bodies of the Tahitian men and women began to disappear, covered by shapeless gowns and stovepipe trousers.

The missionaries did not have it all their own way. As with Brother Veeson in the Friendly Islands the temptation to leave the rather limited life of the Church and join the Tahitians proved strong. A curious tug-of-war developed, with the missionaries urging the Tahitians to emulate them and the islanders coaxing the Europeans to relax a little. The first to do so was John Micklewright, the captain's steward, who "went over" to the Tahitians only two weeks after the arrival of the *Duff* and was given up by the scandalised missionaries. But worse was to befall. One of the four ordained ministers declared that he was going to marry a Tahitian woman. St Paul may have said that it was better to marry than to burn but the missionaries of Tahiti were not so sure. They threatened to excommunicate the Rev. Thomas Lewis, the offending pastor, but to no avail: Lewis went off with his bride. The story had an unhappy ending. Lewis was murdered on 28 November 1799.

Still desertions took place. In 1800 Benjamin Broomhall declared that he had decided he had no immortal soul and was free to do as he pleased. In his case this consisted of going off with one of the willing local beauties. Small wonder that the remaining missionaries became discouraged. One of them wrote in his journal in some gloom of the Tahitians:

> They do not discover the smallest desire to know aught of the things of God; nor have they any curiosity to know why we so frequently meet together to read, sing, and pray; or why we so particularly honour every seventh day, in setting it apart for the worship of God, and refraining from labour thereon. . . .

A more serious event occurred when some of the missionaries tried to prevent the captain of the ship *Nautilus* from selling guns and ammunition to the islanders. Their attempts were unsuccessful but the Christians found themselves embroiled in a desperate situation when a number of the crew deserted. The last thing the missionaries wanted was to have a bunch of renegade Europeans prowling around the island, stirring up trouble and providing the Tahitians with all sorts of bad examples. There had been trouble earlier with a Swedish deserter, but the redoubtable Captain Wilson of the *Duff* had sent him packing. Now the missionaries, led by the Rev. John Jefferson, insisted that Pomare II should hand over the deserters so that they could be returned to their ship. Pomare II did no such thing: instead he stood by while a crowd of Tahitian men attacked Jefferson and three other missionaries and stripped them stark naked. The compassionate old king, Pomare I, saw to it that the Europeans were covered with *tapa,* the local bark-cloth, and returned to the mission station, but the missionaries had been badly shaken. Jefferson himself elected to remain, but eleven of the others had had enough and boarded the *Nautilus* to take passage to Port Jackson in Australia. It was March 1798.

That left seven of the original band of missionaries left in Tahiti. Of the ordained ministers Jefferson and Eyre, together with his wife, remained. There was also Lewis, but he was soon to be lost to the European community. There were also four lay missionaries — Henry Nott, Bicknell, Broomhall and Harris, the latter being the missionary who had had the embarrassing experience in the Marquesas. Broomhall, too, went off with a Ra'iatean wife, and before long Harris left the island altogether.

With only four effective missionaries the outlook was not encouraging, especially as an epidemic, probably of European diseases, was to sweep the island and be blamed on the missionaries. They wrote dolefully in their journal: "They say that if we continue praying and singing, there will not be a chief left alive."

3

BAPTISM OF A KING

The prospect on Tahiti in the Society Islands may have been grim for the missionaries there, but half a world away the officials of the London Missionary Society were relatively undaunted. The evangelistic spirit was strong in Britain at the beginning of the nineteenth century and among its cross-section of Anglicans, Congregationalists, Wesleyans and Presbyterians there were sufficient volunteers from the LMS to replace the defecting missionaries in the South Seas. There were obstacles to be overcome; for example, the *Duff* on her second voyage to Tahiti was captured by a French privateer; but the Society persevered. A training scheme for potential missionaries was drawn up and an agent, Samuel Marsden, appointed to act for the LMS in Australia. It would not be long before reinforcements could be sent to the missionaries who were sticking it out in the Pacific, if only they could wait.

They did. They had little choice. Henry Nott, the former bricklayer, who was emerging as the dominant personality among the Christians, and his colleagues survived local indifference and even open antagonism. On Tahiti they also suffered the scourge of renegade Europeans who were beginning to infest the Pacific islands, so much so that Governor King of New South Wales was driven to complain:

Of late Years there has been a great intercourse with the Society and Sandwich Islands, which has not only furnished them with abundance of Firearms, but has also been the means of a number of Europeans continuing on those Islands, among whom are some of indifferent, not to say bad Characters, mostly left from Ships going to the North-West Coast of America, Whalers and several from this Colony, who have gained much influence with the Chiefs whom they have assisted in their Warfare.

Governor King had cause for concern. Traders, runaway convicts, castaways, and deserters, representing a variety of European nations and America, were to be found in some numbers in New Zealand, Fiji, Tonga, the Society Islands and the Marquesas, engaging in battles with each other and with the islanders. Some of these outcasts joined in the intertribal warfare on Tahiti over the years. The missionaries could do little but watch and deplore.

In 1801 the *Royal Admiral* landed eight more missionaries to join Henry Nott and his companions, and in addition, one or two of the men who had left for Port Jackson returned sheepishly. The Christians were beginning to assemble on Tahiti once more. It was at about this time that they began to conduct their curious love-hate relationship with Pomare II, who became king in 1803. A huge man with enormous appetites, Pomare gave nominal support to the Christians, in return for which he hoped to be supplied with arms and ammunition, but as a heavy-drinking hedonist he was often a cause of considerable embarrassment to Nott and the others.

Extracts from the diaries of the Europeans show that by 1803 they were still making little apparent impression on the Tahitians. One entry records sadly: "When they know that our business is to teach them the word of God, they generally laugh ridicule and tell us that they have heard before and still are not saved, but continue dying, desire us also to look at the crooked backs, scrophulous necks, and on those afflicted by the fever; and tell us that these, with the venereal flux, headache, palpitation of the heart, etc., have all come from England."

It was regrettably true that sailors and other visitors from Europe had introduced all manner of Western diseases to the Society Islands — a shrewd point which the missionaries were hard put to refute. The Christians were also blamed for a number of other catastrophes, in particular the sad case of Brother William Waters. This brother, lately landed from the *Royal Admiral* to bolster the missionary cause, not to put too fine a point upon it went off his head. Among other miscalculations and errors of taste he tried to teach the Tahitians Hebrew and made advances to the queen. His colleagues managed to restrain the ardent brother but the effort taxed even their resources. By this time, however, they were developing a stoical bent. When Brothers William Shelly and John Youl both gave up the ministry to become traders, their former colleagues preserved a tight-

Pomare, King of Tahiti. An engraving, frontispiece to *Polynesian Researches, Volume I,* by William Ellis, 1829.

lipped silence and went about their business. They even survived a lip-smacking scandal when the captain of the *Perseverance* shot himself for the apparently reciprocated love of the bride of one of the newly-arrived brethren.

Throughout all these trials and tribulations the Christian liaison with Pomare II continued to be very much of a mixed blessing. Pomare managed to put down a rising led by a chief named Rua, but at one time it was touch and go. The missionaries, who now depended on the corpulent monarch for their protection, had almost resigned themselves to martyrdom when the fortuitous arrival of two British naval vessels, *Norfolk* and *Venus,* which sent ashore some armed sailors to defend their beleaguered countrymen, saved the day and incidentally put down the uprising.

There were other insurrections, and soon Tahiti became a battle-ground. Pomare clung to the missionaries, professing Christianity and demanding muskets, even writing to the headquarters of the London Missionary Society asking for more missionaries, and going on:

> Friends, send us also property and cloth for us, and we also will adopt English customs. Friends, send also plenty of Muskets and Powder, for wars are frequent in our country. Should I be killed, you will have nothing in Tahete: do not come here when I am dead. . . .

For a long time Pomare could do little against the increasingly victorious rebels. The missionaries, involved against their will in the conflict, saw their houses razed and their goods stolen or destroyed. They fled to the island of Huahine and from there, in 1809, to New South Wales. All except Henry Nott. This stead-fast man, now a master of the local language and engaged on translating passages from the Bible, always exerting pressure on the wilful and petulant Pomare to give up his sinful ways, stayed on Tahiti. He left the island only once, on a romantic mission. The London Missionary Society, ever mindful of the comfort of its charges, had sent to Port Jackson four "godly young women" as brides for the workers in the field. One of the young ladies was for Henry. Nott journeyed to Australia, claimed his bride and returned with her to his work on Tahiti. Some of the missionaries also returned. Pomare was still struggling against his enemies, but the return of the missionaries, with their firearms, was a move in the right direction as far as he was concerned. One attack took place while the king was at a religious service, but those attending rallied to his defence, equipped with guns by the Europeans. As one Tahitian was to write later:

> In the ranks of his followers it was firmly believed that Opuhara [the rebel], few as his forces were, would have won the battle, had not the native missionaries been taught to shoot

as they had been taught to pray, and been given guns along with Bibles.

The alliance with Pomare, star-crossed though it must have seemed at times, eventually paid off; that and the persistence of Henry Nott. Nott was always at the monarch's elbow, nagging, persuading, bullying. It was an odd alliance — the quiet, dedicated missionary and the glutton of a king. Pomare married on a number of occasions, but he was also a homosexual as well as a drunkard; it must sometimes have seemed to the single-minded missionary that he could have been given more promising raw material than Pomare II. Nott persevered, however, and Pomare, in his lucid moments a shrewd and enterprising man, realised that the backing of the Europeans must eventually pay dividends. For his own part, or rather for the mission, Nott had come to a similar conclusion. In the South Sea islands the backing of an influential chief was always going to be essential; Nott appreciated almost from the beginning that the place of the missionaries would have to be somewhere within earshot of the king.

In 1812 Pomare asked for Christian baptism. The effect upon Nott and the other missionaries was rather as if the prodigal son had returned but had brought a few of his dubious city friends with him. There was no doubt that the request marked a turning point in the history of Christianity in the Pacific; with such a powerful king as Pomare in their fold the missionaries would receive many other converts. On the other hand there was the dissolute character of the unreliable monarch to be taken into account. The matter was discussed and prayed over at length. Eventually the missionaries came to a decision. Pomare would be accepted.

The official date of the beginning of the Christian era on Tahiti would be recognised as 12 November 1815 — three years after Pomare had requested Christian baptism. There were a number of reasons for the three-year hiatus. In the first place there was the not unnatural anxiety on the part of Nott and the other Europeans to give the matter the fullest consideration. Pomare, too, had his distractions, mostly in the form of uprisings against his cruel and despotic tactics, and it was not until 1815 that the king routed his final opponent. His magnanimity on this occasion surprised and delighted the missionaries and must have contributed to their decision to accept Pomare for baptism. William Ellis, who arrived at Tahiti several years after Pomare's victory, interviewed survivors and wrote down an account of the king's tolerance after his victory:

> Flushed with success in the moment of victory, the king's warriors were, according to former usage, preparing to pursue the flying enemy. Pomare approached and exclaimed *Atira!* It is enough! — and strictly prohibited any one of his warriors from pursuing those who had fled from the field of battle; forbidding them also to repair to the villages of the vanquished, to plunder their property, or murder their helpless wives and children. . . . not a woman or child was hurt, nor was the property of the vanquished plundered. The bodies of those who fell in the engagement, contrary to the former barbarous practice, were decently buried. . . . In consequence of these events, idolatry was entirely abolished, both at Tahiti and Eimeo . . . the gods are destroyed, the *marais* demolished, human sacrifices and infant murder, we hope, for ever abolished.

It was true that the defeated rebels went over almost *en bloc* to Christianity, but how much of this was owing to genuine conviction and how much to discretion is a moot point. Ellis's claim that the gods were totally abolished was also tinged with optimism. Christianity made enormous strides after Pomare's conversion, but the pagan gods still had their adherents. The priests, described with some vividness by one missionary as "legion fiends of the voluptuous haunts of Belial", continued to claim heavenly origin as descendants of two brothers of Ono, the God of War, though they did not flaunt their presence quite as much as previously.

Even before Pomare's dramatic conversion the missionaries had been making some progress, though it may not have been apparent. As early as 1813 some praying natives had been found, given rudimentary and often inaccurate instruction by former servants of the missionaries, and news of the exploits of the Christians had begun to reach other Pacific islands. The Polynesians had always been renowned for their long sea voyages by canoe, and with the coming of European vessels some had been signing on as deck hands and reaching islands even farther afield. They had taken news of what the Christians were attempting to do on

Tahiti and the other Society Islands. The story of the victory of Pomare and the missionaries over Opuhara had received a particularly wide circulation, and when the LMS eventually went to other islands its work was not completely unknown to some of the inhabitants.

News of the breakthrough on Tahiti was greeted with jubilation in London, especially when it was backed up with a shipment of heathen idols formerly belonging to Pomare and now rejected by the king. A great deal of publicity was given to the success of the missionaries after eighteen years of toil in the Tahitian vineyards. This resulted in a number of gifts of money from impressed laymen and, even more important, of an influx of volunteers to serve in the South Sea Mission. Among them were two men who were to have an enormous impact on Christianity in the Pacific — William Ellis and John Williams. Ellis, a printer who was to become one of the first European scholars in the Pacific (the author of *Polynesian Researches,* London 1829) was to help Nott with the latter's impressive literacy project. Williams became the most successful missionary of his time and the first European after Captain Cook to conduct a practical investigation into the seaways around the central Polynesian islands. He ended his life as a martyr.

Williams was fairly typical of the lower middle class craftsman who made up the field-worker strength of the London Missionary Society. Born in Tottenham High Cross, Middlesex, in 1796, the year in which the *Duff* left on its pioneering missionary voyage to the Pacific, he had been apprenticed at the age of fourteen to a furnishing ironmonger. Williams came of pious parents, but his claim to a godless youth was probably exaggerated. At any rate the turning point of his life came on 30 January 1814, when he was eighteen. He heard Timothy East of Birmingham preaching at the Moorfields Tabernacle, and the sermon so moved him that he joined the Tabernacle, which had strong affiliations with the London Missionary Society. In July 1816 Williams volunteered to be a missionary, passed the examination set by the Society, and was accepted. In November he and his wife and three other missionaries left Britain for Australia on the first part of the journey.

In September 1817 the party left Sydney on board the *Active* for Eimeo, one of the Society Islands, near Tahiti. Ellis had arrived the previous February in the Society Islands. For a while the two men were not particularly noticeable among the many missionaries now returning to Tahiti from Australia or journeying out from England.

By this time Nott, now acknowledged as the senior missionary, was experiencing a particularly busy life. While endeavouring to keep Pomare on the straight and narrow path, he was also engaged in administering the mission, translating the Bible into the local language, teaching Tahitians to read so that they might achieve the benefit of the translations, keeping a wary eye on the political situation, endeavouring to launch various trading ventures to make the mission self-supporting, and doing his best to combat what he regarded as idolatrous ways among the natives. The missionary seems to have been particularly plagued by one of Pomare's *mahoos* or homosexual companions. Writing in his diary at the time, Brother Crook noted:

> Brother Nott reports that when he has gone to the King to translate the Scripture, this vile fellow has lain asleep, and when the King awoke him at one time he was offended and cried like a child. The King then coaxed him and made it up with him. Brother Nott also informed the brethren . . . that he is very near to the King's person, who cannot bear him out of his sight for a minute, and that when he is translating the Scriptures with the King, he (Brother Nott) on one couch and the King on another, this detestable wretch is frequently between them, and he is obliged to turn his head from them to his book to avoid seeing what passes, and still gets his ears shocked with what he hears.

Such annoyances apart, the Christians had some cause for satisfaction by 1819, the year in which Pomare was eventually baptised. Some 200 Tahitians had been formally admitted into the Church and the remainder, as far as could be observed, had largely given up their former pagan practices and were ripe for conversion. Urged on by the missionaries they were giving up their heathen dances and songs. This pleased the Christians immensely, but a number of European visitors noted that in the twenty years or so that the missionaries had been on the island, a lot of the pleasure and light-heartedness seemed to have gone out of the lives of the Tahitians. Some contemporary visitors also faulted the missionaries for encouraging the Tahitians to adopt versions of European dress, and in general for attempting to turn Tahiti into a Pacific version of a Birmingham suburb.

Another portrait of Henry Nott of Tahiti, from the *History of the London Missionary Society 1795-1895, Volume I.* By Richard Lovett, Henry Frowde, London, 1899.

It is true that in Tahiti, as elsewhere in the Pacific, local customs were frowned on by some of the missions, and as a result a great deal of historical value and even aesthetic pleasure was lost; this perhaps is the major charge that can be laid against the first Christians. As for the adoption of European garb, the islanders had started to covet this soon after the arrival of the first sailors from the outside world. Less prominence has been given to the advantages that the missions brought. In the first place there was the word of God, even if it was in the early stages preached by men not ideally suited to the environment in which they found themselves. The islanders were going to have to change anyway. The sailors and traders had landed and brought with them disease, firearms, and the profit-motive. Much as many people may feel that it would have been better for everyone, and certainly for the natives, that the Europeans had never discovered the Pacific islands, the clock was not going to be put back. The Europeans were in the Pacific, and judging by some of the Europeans who were to infest the islands for the rest of the century, it was as well that the missionaries, with all their faults, were there, long before there was any organised law to protect the islanders from the worst excesses of the whalers, sandalwood collectors, slavers and traders. As Robert Louis Stevenson was to write later:

With all their gross blots, with all their deficiency of candour, humour and common sense, the missionaries are the best and most useful whites in the Pacific.

Nott found a most useful ally in William Ellis, who had brought with him a printing press and was able to use it. At last it would be possible to give a wider circulation to those parts of the Bible translated into Tahitian by Nott. Aided by Brother Crook, Ellis set to work with a will, producing a few books and portions of the Bible in Tahitian. The islanders were avid for education. As Ellis wrote, they "learned to read, write, cipher, and commit their lessons to memory with a facility and quickness not exceeded by individuals of the same age in any civilised country".

It is a sign of the new-found confidence of the missionaries that by 1818 they were forming the Tahiti Missionary Society, a local branch of the LMS, with Pomare as its president, to encourage donations of "pigs, or arrow-root, or cocoanut-oil" to be sold to raise funds for missionary activities elsewhere. In the following years the king announced the adoption of eighteen articles, drawn up with the aid of Nott, to deal with various civil transgressions such as theft and murder. While realising the importance of keeping close to the monarch, the missionaries were reluctant to have too much to do with politics; but they realised that if they did so they could ensure some consistency in the laws, and that penalties would not be too severe.

By now Pomare was taking an interest in the non-secular affairs of his kingdom, at least in their outward show. Hearing of the cathedrals of Europe, he ordered a similar building for his own domain. His subjects were pressed into putting up a wooden structure 712 feet long and 54 feet wide, containing 133 windows, 29 doors and 3 pulpits from which 3 preachers could deliver their sermons at the same time.

This incongruous building was followed by the dedication of the church and the long-delayed baptism of the king. The date set for the first occasion was Tuesday, 11 May 1819, and thousands of Tahitians flocked to the new church for the occasion, camping along the beach for miles in both directions. Pomare, suitably decorous for the occasion, was clad in a white shirt and loincloth. The assembly, estimated at 6,000 inside the church and many more unable to gain admittance, joined in hymns in the Tahitian language, prayers and lessons. Then came the three simultaneous sermons. Brother Darling took as his text Isaiah 56:7 ("Even them will I bring to my holy mountain, and make them joyful in my house of prayer."); Brother Platt chose Luke 14:22 ("And he went through the cities and villages, teaching and journeying toward Jerusalem."); Brother Crook adopted Exodus 20:24 ("And Moses said unto the people, Fear not: for God is come to prove you, and that his fear my be before your faces, that ye sin not.").

A week later, in the newly-named Royal Mission Chapel, Pomare II was baptised, seven years after he had first made application, a tribute to his staying power. The ceremony was described by one of the missionaries:

The sight was very moving, especially to our elder brethren, who had been watching over for him so many years. Brother Bicknell addressed the King with firmness, yet not without a large degree of tremour, entreating him to walk worthy of his high profession in the conspicuous situation he holds before the eyes of men, angels and God himself. Brother Henry addressed the people, exhorting them to follow the example of their King, and to give themselves up to the Lord. Another hymn was sung, and Brother Wilson concluded the whole with prayer. Pomare shook hands affectionately with all the missionaries, they being stationed, by his own desire, at his right and left hand.

Alas, it was not long before the monarch was backsliding, to the despair of his missionary friends. A year later Baron Thaddeus Bellingshausen, a Russian navigator visited Tahiti. The baron commented on the fact that human sacrifice, tribal wars and infanticide seemed to have been put aside by the Tahitians and that the people, though still cheerful, had been Europeanised to the extent of cutting their hair, giving up their garlands of flowers, observing the Sabbath and actually working — having established a coconut oil industry. The more important islanders were now living in enclosed wooden houses and sleeping on beds, rather than inhabiting huts open to the wind and sleeping on the floor.

Pomare, however, appears to have been as much a reprobate as ever. One day Bellingshausen visited the king in the company of Henry Nott. The baron noted:

> I noticed that the presence of Mr Nott was unwelcome to the King, and that he hastened to close the door. He then showed me his clock, his map, his copy-book, and the elementary principles of geometry, which he was studying with the help of an English book, which he understood, transcribing it into the copy-book in the Otahitan tongue. From the book he took an inkstand, a pen and a few scraps of paper, which he gave to me, asking me to write in Russian that the bearer of the note should be given a bottle of rum. I wrote to the effect that he should be given three bottles of rum and six bottles of Teneriffe wine. At this moment Mr Nott and Mr Lalarev came in. The King looked confused, hid the note and changed the conversation to his ink, paper and geometry book.

When Pomare died in 1821 some of the missionaries were at his bedside. He left behind him an infant son whom the missionaries promised to look after. William Ellis described the funeral and could not prevent an element of bitterness entering his tone:

> Brother Nott addressed the people at the grave, after which the soldiers fired, and the vessels in Wilks' Harbour fired minute guns. The Queen provided a dinner in the European style, having borrowed plates, etc. and the gentlemen from the ship furnished her with wine. This was advancing a step in civilization beyond anything we had seen with the King.

The missionaries took an early opportunity of crowning the young king, who was about four years old at the death of his father. Needless to say the coronation was conducted in accordance with the strictest Christian principles. The young king sat before a number of small tables bearing the crown, a Bible, and a copy of the laws. The crown was placed on the infant's head by Henry Nott. As a sign of their interest the missionaries allowed him to attend the South Sea Academy on the island of Eimeo, an educational institution reserved as a rule for their own children. Unfortunately the child was never to repay the missionaries for their consideration, for in 1827 he died of dysentery.

At the time of the young king's death the missionaries were well in command. Their jurisdiction was recognised by Governor

William Ellis. An engraving, frontispiece to *Narrative of a tour through Hawaii . . .* , by William Ellis, London, 1827.

King who had appointed one of them a Justice of the Peace, admitting that the only law on the island was that administered by the missionaries. The economy, such as it was, had also largely been taken over by the representatives of the LMS. As early as 1817 they had gone into partnership with Pomare II in the building of a seventy-ton trading vessel. The idea had been to collect pearls and mother-of-pearl from the Tuamotu Islands and to convey them to the rapidly-developing colony of New South Wales, where the cargo would be exchanged for various manufactured goods. The missionaries hoped that the islanders would so covet the knives, tools, and other supplies brought back in the trading ship that they would even be willing to work to earn money to buy such things. In order to meet the hoped-for demand for work the missionaries set up a number of embryonic industries — a sugar mill, a cotton mill equipped with weaving and spinning machines, and the collection of coconut oil.

The trading vessel was not a success. Neither were the industries. The ship named the *Haweis* after Dr Haweis who had helped to found the LMS, ran into trouble even at the launching ceremony when the breaking of a bottle of wine over the bows so intrigued the islanders who were manoeuvring the vessel down the launching slope that they dropped their ropes. The ship ran unchecked into the water and almost sank. For a time the *Haweis* monopolised the energies of the missionaries, occupying most of their time as they tried to maintain their venture on an even commercial keel. It was not to be, however, and the ship was sold after several disappointing trading voyages.

The sugar mill was equally disheartening. Brothers Darling and Platt did their best, but they chose for an overseer (or had chosen for them) a gentleman whose previous experience had been in driving slave labour in the West Indies. Even the easy-going Tahitians were not going to accept the boot and the lash and before very long the overseer left. The mill kept going for a time, but there was never a sugar-exporting industry on Tahiti.

The cotton mill got off to a better start, for the Tahitians were intrigued by the spinning and weaving machines and eagerly learnt to operate them. When it became apparent that they were expected to work these machines day in and day out, however, their enhusiasm cooled and another missionary project vanished. This did not worry all the brothers, for some of them had become a little concerned about this new emphasis on local industries. One had even commented vehemently: "We are a set of trading priests, our closets are neglected, and our cloth disgraced."

The officials of the LMS in London were also a little apprehensive about the deep interest their Pacific representatives were still taking in Tahiti, to the apparent neglect of other island groups. Considering that the island was now emphatically Christian and that missionaries had been in residence on it for over twenty years, it was felt that perhaps there should be occasional moves to other parts of the Pacific. Fortunately both William Ellis and John Williams had the same idea and in 1818 they sailed from Eimeo to Huahine, north-west of Tahiti. With them went their wives and a number of other missionaries and their wives. The inhabitants of Huahine had already received word of what had happened on Tahiti. One expedition from there had returned from

The destruction of idols at Tahiti. A woodcut from *Missionary Sketches, VI,* July 1819.

Tahiti with the words: "We are all praying people and have become worshippers of the living and true God." These converts had brought back copies of books sent by the missionaries. Not all the inhabitants were happy about the conversion of some of their number, but after some dissension it was agreed to send to Tahiti and ask for instructors in the new religion. Williams and Ellis led the first party. Within a year a church, school, carpenter's shop and forge had all been built or almost constructed.

Other islanders had heard of Tahiti's conversion to the European religion. John Williams, exhibiting the restlessness that characterised him, was eager to take the word of God to some of them. His chance came after he had been only a few months on Huahine. Tamatoa, king of Raiatea in the Society Islands, asked Williams and Lancelot Threlkeld, another missionary, to visit his island. Williams and his colleague accepted. Native teachers were beginning to visit other isolated islands with their messages. By 1820 Christianity was about to spread to many parts of the Pacific.

4

CAN THEY BE CHRISTIANISED?

The work of the representatives of the London Missionary Society was receiving plenty of publicity. The Society itself issued pamphlets, extracts from diaries, sermons, and articles describing the work taking place in Tahiti, and these received a wide circulation. Some of them reached America where they were greatly discussed. It was felt that an American equivalent of the LMS should be formed, and in 1810 at a meeting of the Congregationalist General Association the American Board of Commissioners for Foreign Missions was established. The Rev. Adoniram Judson, was sent to London to learn what he could from the LMS, but any plans for sending him to the Pacific came to nothing and the missionary eventually went to work in Burma.

For some time the American Board of Missions languished. Then it was given an impetus by the arrival in the USA of a number of youths from the Sandwich Islands, or Hawaii. These islands had been discovered by Captain Cook, and the famous explorer had in fact met his death there at the hands of the islanders, but not before he had been taken for a god. The islands had then been left in peace for some time, but American whalers had taken to visiting Hawaii and had recruited a number of islanders as deckhands. In 1811 the Sandwich Islands had become the centre of a sandalwood boom and various islanders had shipped on these vessels.

It had only been a matter of time before some of the Hawaiians reached North America. In 1809 two were brought to New Haven by a returning sea captain and were made much of by the faculty at Yale. Both youths were subjected to a variety of Christian teaching, and one in particular seemed to take to his new faith with such alacrity that the thought of thousands like him waiting to be converted in the Sandwich Islands attracted a number of laymen and ministers. In 1817 a school for heathen youths was opened at Cornwall in Connecticut. Seven of the first dozen students were Hawaiians.

This revival of interest in missions to the Pacific was taken advantage of by the American Board of Missions and missionaries were selected to go to Hawaii. Only two of the original band were ordained ministers, Hiram Bingham and Asa Thurston. Some laymen accompanied them — three schoolmasters, Samuel Ruggles, Elisha Loomis and Samuel Whitney, and one physician, Dr Thomas Holman. All the missionaries took their wives, those previously unmarried being encouraged to wed before the journey. Three or four Hawaiians from the school in Cornwall went with the party.

Many gifts in money and kind were presented to the missionaries, including a frame house, a rocking chair and several hundred copies of the Bible. Particular interest was aroused in New England, probably because the expedition gathered at Boston for three days of prayer and sermonising before sailing on 23 October 1819. They left in the brig *Thaddeus*. The voyage out was memorable chiefly for the sight of a number of sharks and the fact that Brother Whitney managed to fall overboard while painting the side of the ship. He managed to pull himself on to a bench thrown over the side to him and was picked up wet, exhausted, and praying furiously. Hawaii was reached without further excitement by the end of March 1820 after a voyage of five months. In rather lush prose Bingham described the scene from the deck of the *Thaddeus* as the missionaries and their wives stared ashore:

The appearance of destitution, degradation, and barbarism among the chattering and almost naked savages, whose heads and feet, and much of their sunburned swarthy skins, were bare, was appalling. Some of our number, with gushing tears, turned away from the spectacle. Others with firmer nerve continued their gaze, but were ready to exclaim, 'Can these be human beings.' How dark and comfortless their state of mind and heart! How imminent the danger to the immortal soul, shrouded in this deep pagan gloom! Can such things be civilized? Can they be Christianized? Can we throw ourselves upon these rude shores, and take up our abode, for life, among such people, for the purpose of training them for Heaven?'

The Hawaiians greeted them courteously, far more courteously,

The Rev. Mr Alexander preaching in a grove of tutui trees, Kauai, Hawaiian Islands. An engraving after A. T. Agate, in *Narrative of the United States Exploring Expedition, Vol IV*, by Charles Wilkes, USN, 1845.

judging by Bingham's monologue, than they deserved. It seemed, however, that the Americans had arrived at an opportune time. The new king, Kamehameha II, had decreed that the old idolatrous worship should cease. Human sacrifices had been a part of this system and for the most part the Hawaiians were not sorry to see an end to such a cruel form \of worship. They were less willing to give up other aspects of their lives, characterised, perhaps with some exaggeration, by the puritanical Bingham as: "Polygamy, fornication, adultery, incest, infant murder, desertion of husbands and wives, parents and children, sorcery, covetousness and oppression. . . ."

King Kamehameha received the missionaries at Kailua. He was polite but the Americans found him to be no tremulous savage; indeed, he was not at all sure that he wanted the missionaries on Hawaii, even though they had given him a presentation copy of the Bible. The Americans had to use all their powers of persuasion and the liberal distribution of many gifts before Kamehameha and his advisers could be persuaded to grant them a probationary year in the Sandwich Islands. One of the factors favouring the final decision was that the king recognised the advantage of having in Holman a qualified doctor.

The missionaries were split up among the different islands. Though engaged in building houses and growing food, as well as in learning the language, they began to conduct services. They had taken a printing press with them and began to develop a written form of the Hawaiian language and then produced books, having first, of course, to teach the islanders to read and write. Some of the chiefs were so enthusiastic about this that one of them forbade his people to marry unless they were literate.

Three years after their arrival the Americans were reinforced by the sudden appearance of the ubiquitous William Ellis from Tahiti. He stayed with them for several years and travelled about the Sandwich Islands, helping individual missionaries before returning to Britain. Less helpful European visitors were sailors from whalers and trading vessels, eager for the charms of the Hawaiian women. The missionaries had done their best to stamp out the cheerful brand of prostitution practised on Hawaii and this did not endear them to the seamen. Some of the missionaries were assaulted by the crew of the US naval vessel *Dolphin* and for safety's sake were forced to lift for ten weeks the ban on Hawaiian women visiting ships in the harbour.

The missionaries on the Sandwich Islands soon adopted the tactics pursued earlier by those on Tahiti. It was obvious that if Christianity was to spread and fill the void left by the abandoning of the old religion, the important chiefs would have to be cultivated. To this end the missionaries opened a special school for the high-born where they taught reading and writing. Among those interested was Keopuolani, the mother of the king and a woman of great influence. She grew to like the missionaries and ordered her subjects to build two houses and a church for them. Before she died in 1823 she asked for a Christian baptism which was given to her by William Ellis, the American missionaries not yet being proficient enough in the Hawaiian language. Another important convert was the dowager regent Kaahumanu who ruled while the king and queen were in England, where they both died. When Kaahumanu announced that she had become a Christian many chiefs hurried to announce their conversions as well. By

The Lahainaluna seminary about 1838. An engraving on copper held in the Alexander Turnbull Library (Wellington) Art Collection.

1825, after only six years of effort, the missionaries on Hawaii seemed well on their way to success.

At about this time there had been another attempt to establish Christianity on Tonga in the Friendly Islands, this time by the Wesleyans. The General Wesleyan Missionary Society had been formed in 1817 and in 1822 it found a missionary prepared to go to the South Sea as an apostle of Methodism. The volunteer was Walter Lawry, an ordained minister who had heard a great deal about the attempt of the LMS to establish a mission on Tonga from the widow of Shelly, one of the original missionaries, who had settled in New South Wales. Lawry, convinced that he had experienced a call to the Friendly Isles, persuaded the British Conference of 1820 to send two ministers to Tonga, one of them to be himself. Eager to get to work he left before the other missionary could join him, and reached Tonga, landing at Mu'a on 16 August 1822, bringing with him his wife, two artisans and some cattle, a present from the Governor of Brisbane.

Fatu, one of the chiefs, gave Lawry some land, but the heathen priests saw that if Christianity took hold their own days would be numbered. They campaigned against the minister, insinuating that he was a spy come to report on the state of the land before other white men arrived and took it away from them. While most of the Tongans were fairly tolerant, some of them were driven by the priests to steal from Lawry and his wife and generally make their lives a misery. After fourteen months Mr Lawry felt she could stand the persecution no longer and she and her husband sailed sorrowfully away from Tonga, on 3 October 1823. Ironically, a young chief named Futakava returned from a visit to Sydney just before Lawry left and reported that the people of New South Wales seemed friendly and devout and that perhaps the Tongans should give some consideration to adopting the Christian religion. By that time the Lawrys had determined to go and Mrs Lawry could not be persuaded to change her mind.

Lawry continued to harbour feelings of goodwill towards the Tongans and often preached about his days there, keeping the islands in the minds of mission officials in Britain and Australia. In 1826 two Tahitian missionaries, forerunners of many of their kind who had been trained at Tahiti by European ministers of the LMS called at Tonga on their way to Fiji. Their names were Habe and Tafeta. One of the Tongan chiefs, Aleamotu'a, persuaded them to stay and teach the Tongans about the Christian God. They agreed, and in a remarkable campaign managed to interest some 300 Tongans in their religion, a church being specially built for them at Nuku'alofa where regular worship took place.

In the same year two white missionaries arrived, sent by the Wesleyans to replace the departed Lawry. They were John Thomas and John Hutchinson, and they landed at Maria Bay on 28 June 1826, being met by a white former servant of Lawry's who had remained on one of the islands of the group. This man advised the missionaries against going on to their intended destination of Mu'a, so they settled at Ha'atafu where they were given land by a chief called Ata. But this chief would not allow any of his people to be converted, and though hospitable enough treated the missionaries with caution. This was understandable because on Tonga, as on many other islands, Europeans were becoming objects of great hostility. The sandalwood traders had made their name a byword for cruelty and deception, and the deserted seamen and escaped convicts were imposing reigns of terror in a number of areas. Visiting European vessels were also treated with great suspicion, and not without cause: in 1827 the French navigator d'Urville had bombarded one of the islands of Tonga for two days after sailors from his vessel, the *Astrolabe,* had fallen out with the Tongans. A visit from the Irish trader Peter Dillon had also sparked off antagonism.

Through all these distractions Thomas and his colleague wearily attempted to do their work. They were assisted by the Tahitian teachers from the LMS, who put aside all thought of sectarianism in their efforts to bring Christianity to Tonga. The missionaries found their progress heartbreakingly slow. At one point Thomas despaired and decided to emulate Lawry and return home, going so far as to send some of his possessions back to Australia with a letter begging to be allowed to return himself. Fortunately for the sake of the Wesleyans, the letter was seen by Nathaniel Turner, a former missionary in New Zealand who happened to be in Sydney when his colleague's letter arrived. Turner could appreciate Thomas's feelings as he had himself been rejected by the Maoris in New Zealand. He determined that on this occasion the mission should dig in its heels and fight for the souls of the Tongans. Accordingly Turner left Australia to join Thomas, accompanied by another missionary, William Cross. Somewhere the missions were always able to find men prepared to journey into the unknown.

Turner and Cross arrived in the Friendly Islands in 1828, and the former became the head of the mission. They settled at Nuku'alofa under the protection of the chief Aleamotua. Turner, a man of some firmness and strength of character, saw that Thomas was getting nowhere with the obdurate Ata. There seemed to be much more promising material in the Ha'apai Islands where the chief Taufa'ahau was known to be growing interested in Christianity. He had been caught in a dangerous storm at sea which seemed to have convinced him that the Christian God had a great deal to offer, and he received some instruction from a

A battle between the pinnace of the Astrolabe and the natives of Tonga. A lithograph after de Sainson, in *Dumont D'Urville: Voyage de l'Astrolabe . . . Vol I, 1826-29.*

young Tongan Christian in the new religion. Taufa'ahau made a runaway European sailor teach him to write by scratching the letters of the alphabet in the sand. When Thomas arrived on the chief's island he found him prepared to listen, which was all that the missionary required. Strength was added to the Wesleyan's case when Taufa'ahau fell ill (or was poisoned) and then recovered, attributing his recovery to the Christian God.

It was as if a wedge holding back a huge boulder had been removed. With Taufa'ahau showing interest and even some limited enthusiasm for Christianity, his people began to be interested. Soon there was a minor landslide of evangelism on the island. By 1830 Thomas, who had been joined by Cross, was working hard and successfully. Taufa'ahau, while still retaining too many of his pagan ways for the missionaries' liking, was certainly a powerful ally. A man of considerable perception, as well as a brave and enterprising leader, Taufa'ahau was quick to see that unless they united, the scattered islands and numerous chiefs of the Tongan group could do little against the increasing inroads of the Europeans. During a long lifetime he did much to ensure the ultimate independence of the Friendly Islands. It was Taufa'ahau who saw that the pagan ways of the past could not be carried into the new age dawning in the Pacific. The Tongans would have to adapt, but turning to Christianity was mainly an expediency as far as he was concerned. He realised, as Pomare II in Tahiti had realised, that of all the invading Europeans the missionaries were the least dangerous and grasping, the only white men who seemed willing to do something for the islanders. An alliance with them against the traders and other marauding Europeans was something to be desired. Nothing in the chief's actions indicate that he had any real conception of the faith he was willing to adopt, but the missionaries were not too worried. Like their spiritual brothers in the Society Islands, they had concluded that the way to the people lay through their chiefs.

The Wesleyans were beginning to make progress among the Friendly Islands: in 1828 they opened their first schools — for a hundred years and more education in the South Pacific was to come mainly from the Churches; on 9 January 1829 the Wesleyans conducted their first baptism outside their stronghold of Nuku'alofa, when Lolohea, the son of Tubouniua, an important leader, became a Christian; in 1831 a printing press was set up and the first books printed in the Friendly Islands.

There was still a great deal of opposition to the new faith, mainly from the pagan priests and from minor chiefs jealous of Taufa'ahau, who it must be admitted had done a great deal to incur enmity by breaking idols and smashing the priests' meeting places with undue severity. Such an attitude had its effect, however, because much of Tonga was inclining towards Christianity, or at least Taufa'ahau's version of it, even before the European missionaries first visited him. Some of the credit for the leader's conversion must go to a Tongan missionary, Peter (or Bita) Vi. At first Taufa'ahau had refused to be taught by another Tongan but eventually relented.

At one stage his enemies even managed to poison him, but Thomas was sent for and managed to cure the stricken chief when his family had despaired of his life. In 1831 Taufa'ahau and three of his children were baptised, the chief taking the name George in honour of King George III of Great Britain. This gave the missionaries a great deal of prestige among the islands and they continued to visit as many in the group as possible. On one trip in 1832, while attempting to get to Vava'u, the boat carrying the missionaries was wrecked and Mrs Cross was drowned.

Such tragedies were to be common among the missionaries, but they did not deter them for some time. By 1835 they had made giant strides, but they were to need all their new-found strength, for a large-scale civil war was looming up, and those missionaries who remembered the fate of their LMS colleagues who had become embroiled in a similar disorder at the end of the eighteenth century wondered what disasters the new war would bring.

The American Board of Missions in Hawaii and the Wesleyans in Tonga were carrying on the work started by the representatives of the London Missionary Society in Tahiti, but the LMS, after a period of torpor, was no longer resting on its oars. With the arrival of William Ellis and John Williams the Society had greatly increased its range. Ellis had done his best to help the Americans on Hawaii and had then returned to London where his books became enormously successful and gave the missionaries in the Pacific much publicity.

Apart from one four-year spell in the United Kingdom, Williams spent the rest of his life in the Pacific, visiting in an amazing eighteen-year period Rarotonga, Tahiti, the Cooks, Tonga, Fiji, Samoa, the New Hebrides and other islands. A practical but restless man, Williams did good work wherever he landed, but he seldom stayed long in one place, preferring to let other missionaries develop the area he had first evangelised. He was a great believer in trade as an adjunct to Christianity, convinced that if the islanders were provided with work they would have less time to get into mischief. Such an attitude, adopted by most missionaries, was strongly backed in Britain, which was one reason why missionary work was regarded with such favour by the Government. The preachers, it was believed with some truth, were opening up new markets for British trade. A number of missionaries in the process became wealthy men, a fact seized upon by their adversaries, particularly by the traders with whom they came into competition.

These commercial traders were to become bitter enemies, partly because the missionaries themselves were engaging in trade, but also because their presence prevented the worst excesses of the less honest commercial representatives in the area. After 1800 there were many such. Whales were hunted by the Americans, British, and French. Sandalwood, in great demand for incense in China, commanded high prices as did *bêche-de-mer,* the sea slug considered a great delicacy by the Chinese. Turtle shell and mother-of-pearl fetched high prices also.

Normally, the traders of the Pacific used Australia or Hawaii as their headquarters in the early years of the century. Some were men of honesty and compassion, the majority were not. Ruthless in search of profit, they descended on the islands like wolves. The sandalwood traders were particularly feared and hated. As soon as it had been discovered that great forests of sandalwood trees grew on some of the Pacific islands the traders made for them. The trees were felled and carried back to the ships and any native who protested was beaten up or killed. At the beginning of the nineteenth century Fiji was the first to suffer the attentions of the sandalwood men, and within fifteen years there were hardly any sandalwood trees remaining. Then for ten years it was the turn of Hawaii and the Marquesas. By 1820 the traders, leaving destruction behind them like a swarm of locusts, had reached the New Hebrides and other islands in the South Pacific.

There was little in the way of law with which to threaten them. Cutting down trees and killing their owners became an accepted way of life for the sandalwood men, until in many areas, particularly the fiercer parts of Melanesia, the Europeans were greeted on the beaches by warriors determined to stop their homes being pillaged. Sometimes the islanders drove off the sailors, but more often the superior firepower of the Europeans won the day. The missionaries complained loudly about the behaviour of their commercial compatriots, to little avail. The only hope lay in occasional vessels of the Royal Navy touring among the islands, but these were few and far between and the powers of their officers severely limited. They could arrest European offenders but not try them. Two Acts, one in 1824 and the other in 1829, gave the Supreme Court of New South Wales the power to try British subjects who had committed serious offences — murder, assault, and so on — in the Pacific, but in the early rough-and-ready days of the colony, sympathy tended to be on the side of the transgressors and not of authority, especially when that authority was wielded by the British Navy. As late as 1848 Earl Grey at the Colonial Office was writing of the "anxious desire of Her Majesty's Government to do all in their power to prevent the ill-treatment of the natives of the islands in the Pacific by British subjects", but in 1870 and later British naval officers were still getting scant support in the courts of New South Wales when they brought in malcontents arrested in the Pacific.

This then was the situation with which John Williams had to contend during his epic voyages among the Polynesian islands between 1817 and 1839. He was seldom the first white man to visit an island — usually the traders had been there before him — and often resentment and antagonism had to be overcome before he could make a start.

For a time, however, Williams must have wondered if he was ever going to be allowed to make that start. Six months after his arrival in Tahiti he had arranged to be sent to Huahine and then, three months later, on to Raiatea where he laboured mightily,

"The author's [i.e. John William's] residence at Raiatea, after the model of which Mr Pitman's was built." "Mr Buzacott's residence, an imitation of which the king's was built." Williams's house was at Raiatea, Buzacott's at Rarotonga. The engravings by G. Baxter in *A narrative of missionary enterprises in the South Sea Islands,* by John Williams, 1837.

urging the islanders to build him a house and then encouraging them, with the help of convict labour, to construct a system of roads about the island. With the assistance of Brother Threlkeld he also set about converting the chief, an object accompanied with surprising ease, doubtless owing something to Williams's single-minded pursuance of an objective.

A church, complete with chandeliers, was built by the natives, who probably did not know what had hit them. Nor did Williams neglect the commercial aspect of missionary life. By 1821 the London Missionary Society was making a profit of £1,800 a year from a Raiatean coconut oil industry. This was enough as far as John Williams was concerned; he had evangelised the island and turned a neat profit for the mission in the process. Some of the other brothers could take up the torch: it was time John Williams moved on. He wrote to London and said as much to the elders of the Society: "I cannot content myself within the narrow limits of a single reef," he declared. The answer was a dusty one, for the gentlemen at headquarters were not accustomed to being so importuned by junior missionaries. They had no intention of providing a ship for the restless young man to enable him to sail off into the blue.

Then, by a stroke of fate, the mountain came to Mahomet (though this analogy would never have been considered by the puritanical Williams). He could not get out to the heathen, but some of the heathen came to him. In March 1821 a boatload of islanders from Rurutu in the Austral group, blown off course, landed on Raiatea. Williams was delighted to greet them and saw to it that they were well looked after, and as soon as they had recovered he talked to them. It was the first of many similar visits. Williams treated the Rurutuans kindly and they in turn were impressed by the Englishman, his church and especially its chandeliers. Raiatean teachers were allocated to the visitors to teach the elements of Christianity and the rudiments of reading and writing. Before they returned to their own island all the men of Rurutu had been converted to Christianity. Some/time after they had left Raiatea they delighted Williams by sending him a boatload of their old idols, for which they had no further use.

In 1821 Williams's wife became ill and it was decided that he should take her to Sydney for treatment. Never a man to let an opportunity slip, he gathered together some religious tracts and a number of Raiatean converts who had volunteered to act as missionaries to other islands. This was the beginning of one of the most important phases of missionary work in the South Sea, the evangelising of islanders by other islanders. Fortunately for Williams the vessel on which he took passage to New South Wales with his wife was captained by a man of Christian leanings who was willing to make one or two detours in order to visit some of the relatively unknown islands en route.

Their first stop was at Aitutaki in the Cook Islands. Here the islanders had already heard of Christianity and seemed favourably disposed towards Williams and the native teachers. Encouraged by this reception he left the two Raiatean teachers there and proceeded to Sydney. With great coolness, while his wife was undergoing treatment, Williams negotiated to buy a vessel; borrowing the money, he explained that it would be operated by himself and the chiefs of Raiatea and some of the surrounding islands in the Society group, and that he would guarantee a profitable trading run between this group and Sydney.

A man who could persuade the natives of Raiatea to build him a house would have found the merchants of Sydney mere child's play. The money was produced, a schooner purchased and Williams sailed from Sydney in 1822. On his way back to Raiatea he called in at Aitutaki to find that his Raiatean missionaries had been doing sterling work. They had built a church, converted a number of the islanders and collected a donation of £66 from a shipwrecked trader, thus fulfilling all Williams's demands of building, proselytism, and fund-raising. It might be objected that his attitude was excessively hard-headed but it is a fact that he survived and established Christianity among the islands where less business-minded men failed abysmally.

Greatly satisfied with the progress being made at Aitutaki, Williams sailed back to Raiatea where he spent the greater part of the year in administering, with some reluctance, his flock, while other missionaries went to Rurutu to carry on the work he had started. His turn was to come. Now he owned, or partly-owned his own vessel, the *Endeavour*. With this means of escape his superiors could not keep him pinned down, not, to do them justice, that they tried very hard to do so after the initial refusal.

The hierarchy of the LMS realised that in Williams they had an exceptional young man and one who would work best if allowed his head.

In July 1823 John Williams left Raiatea on the *Endeavour*, taking with him some native teachers and their wives, religious texts, and trading goods. His first destination was to be Aitutaki. Then he wanted to search for the island of Rarotonga, an island of which Williams had heard and which he wanted to evangelise.

Aitutaki was reached without incident and he discovered that good progress had been made by the Raiatean teachers. Many of the islanders were observing the Sabbath, a number had learned to read, and some had committed portions of the catechism to memory. Pausing only to preach a fiery sermon, Williams took on board some Rarotongan converts and set out to search for their home island, which for some reason had fired his imagination.

The next island they came across, however, was Mangaia in the Cooks. Here the missionaries were not well-received and Williams, mentally marking the island down for conversion at some future date, sailed on in his quest for Rarotonga, which was reached some days later. At first the visiting party was greeted hospitably by the Rarotongans and a number of Raiatean teachers and their wives went ashore. Then things began to go wrong. On board the *Endeavour* had been a young Rarotonga woman, Tapaeru, who had been shipwrecked on Aitutaki and converted to Christianity before being returned to her home island on the vessel. The Rarotongans threw a big party to welcome Tapaeru back. At the height of the festivities many of the guests became extremely drunk, and King Makea made advances to the wives of the Raiatean missionaries, and when repulsed became annoyed. His anger spread to his subjects, who turned on the missionaries and beat them badly, though Tapaeru did her best to prevent it. At dawn the Raiateans ran back to the beach, badly bruised, and managed to get back on the *Endeavour*. Williams, who had not gone ashore, had given the order for the anchor to be raised when Papeiha, a Raiatean bachelor teacher, stepped forward and volunteered to go ashore, face the angry mob, and endeavour to stay with the Rarotongans as their teacher.

Williams was much impressed by this gesture, later writing, "instead of uniting with us in our useless regrets, [he] resolved

Papeiha, a Raiatean bachelor teacher, who volunteered to stay with the Rarotongans as their missionary. From the *History of the London Missionary Society, 1795-1895, Volume I,* by Richard Lovett, Henry Frowde, London, 1899.

to be left to attempt the work". It was certainly a most courageous act and one which contrasts with the rather tawdry tales of islanders adopting Christianity for utilitarian and political reasons. There must have been many others like the young Papeiha, men who really believed in their new faith and were willing to prove it in no uncertain manner. Advancing to the side of the vessel, Papeiha declared that whether the Rarotongans spared him or killed him he would land among them. Shouting *"Ko Jehova toku tiaki! Tei roto au i tona rima!"* ("Jehovah is my shepherd! I am in His hand!"), the young Raiatean, clad only in a shirt and a few yards of calico, tied a book containing passages of the Holy Scripture in Tahitian into a handkerchief, jumped over the side into the sea, and began to swim for the shore. Williams and the others watched him go. Papeiha reached the shore and disappeared among the Rarotongans assembled there. Sadly Williams ordered the *Endeavour* to be sailed away. He prayed for the safety of the young missionary but secretly considered his chances of survival almost non-existent.

As it turned out, the story of Papeiha on Rarotonga became one of the greatest and strangest in the annals of the London Missionary Society. When the young Raiatean landed on the beach some of the islanders wanted to kill him, but Tapaeru pleaded for his life. The king agreed to allow him to live under his protection, but laughed at the missionary's declaration that he would overthrow the gods of Rarotonga.

Yet that is what the young man proceeded to do. An account of his work, sponsored by the LMS and published in 1856 a little over twenty years after he had landed at Rarotonga and while he was still alive and his exploits fresh in people's minds, says:

From the first day of his landing Papeiha gave himself solely to his work; every act of his daily life stood out in bold contrast with the deeds of the people. Whether at home or abroad, whether at meals or work, he was at all times surrounded by a number of natives, curious to see and hear some new thing. As his actions and words were reported from clan to clan, crowds of people came from all parts of the island, to whom he gave a simple exposition of the great design of the "Evangelia a Jesu", and narrated to each party details respecting the overthrow of heathenism and idolatory in the Tahitian Islands.

The news that the missionaries had stopped all war in Tahiti, an over-optimistic forecast as it turned out, amazed the fierce Rarotongans. So many of them flocked to hear Papeiha that it became necessary to look for a more formal meeting-place. A grove among palm trees was selected, and every day the Raiatean missionary held a meeting there, talking to the people and reading to them from the Holy Scriptures, which many took to be the God he was talking about. From holding services the amazing Papeiha went on to establish a school at which he taught both children and adults the Tahitian alphabet and the fundamentals of reading and writing.

After a while one chief, Tinomana, began to show a nervous interest in Christianity. Papeiha redoubled his efforts and persuaded him to destroy his idols. Greatly daring, the chief did so and marvelled to find himself still alive. Other chiefs followed his example. Papeiha was beginning to make progress, but it was slow work: a church he built was destroyed in a storm, which many took to be a judgment on the Christians, and the houses of some Rarotongan converts were burned by pagan priests. But the missionary and his converts survived.

It was four years before John Williams returned, but the delay had not been of his choosing. On his return to Raiatea he had survived the almost crushing blow of being forced to sell the *Endeavour:* this was caused by the imposition of a set of punitive customs duties on goods imported from the Polynesian islands, set by the authorities in New South Wales. The missionary complained vehemently but could do nothing. He had opened the door only to

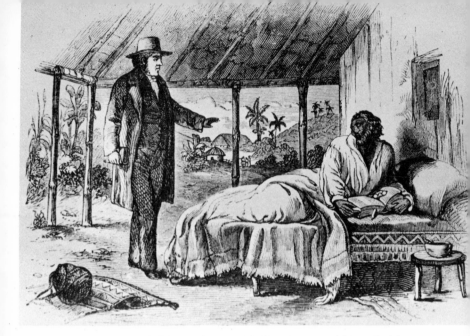

"What! All alone, Tinomana?" "No, I am not alone; God is here." An engraving in *Gems from the Coral Islands, Volume II,* by the Rev. William Gill, Ward & Co. London, 1956. Tinomana, Chief of Aorangi, a district of Rarotonga, was the first chief on the island to destroy his idols. During his last illness the Rev. A. Buzacott often visited him (sketch). Tinomana died in 1854, aged 70, "his heart fixed on God".

have it slammed shut in his face again. It almost seemed as if he was fated to remain on Raiatea. To make things more galling other missionaries were beginning to open up new territories. In the Australs Rurutu and Rimitara had both been visited by other European missionaries. Williams felt that he had been left behind.

For two years, however, he had been teaching two Europeans, Charles Pitman, a minister, and his wife, preparing them for pastoral work on Rarotonga. By 1827 Williams decided that the Pitmans were ready and that it was his bounden duty to conduct them to the island. Delegating his work on Raiatea to a local deacon, he set out on a trading vessel with the Pitmans for Rarotonga.

Although he was always eager to be off to fresh pastures, it should not be deduced that Williams skimped his pastoral duties. Writing in 1825 he gives an account of his daily labours:

Our daily employment is as follows: Every morning, Saturday excepted, at school from six o'clock to eight. Monday evening we have conversation meetings; Wednesday evening, preaching; Friday evening, we have a full meeting of the members and the baptized, when, after singing, prayer, and a short exhortation, the natives speak . . . On Saturday, the judicial proceedings of the week are settled, which generally occupy two or three hours . . . On Sabbath days, you know, perhaps, that we are fully employed. The natives, at six o'clock, hold a prayer meeting. At nine o'clock we have regular service. After this, Mrs. Williams reads aloud some interesting work for our spiritual edification, except any vessels are here, when I always preach in English. At one o'clock the bell rings again, when we have a kind of catechetical service on the sermon preached in the forenoon. In the afternoon there is another regular service. . . .

All this and a regular routine of house- and road-building, coconut oil trading, farming and fishing! It was small wonder that the energetic Williams became something of a legend in his own lifetime. On the voyage back to Rarotonga he was as lively as ever and the Pitmans, if they had not already done so, must have become reconciled to the knowledge that as long as John Williams was with them he was going to be the dominant personality on their new mission station. They appear to have been a tolerant and good-natured pair, or else subdued by the sheer driving force of their colleague's personality, because they bore their role with grace and discretion.

Papeiha had done his work well and the Rarotongans welcomed the European missionaries. Williams set to work at once, and within six months was able to report with a touch of self-righteousness:

. . . peace and good-will prevail throughout the island. I have also prepared a very long account of the islands, gods, introduction of Christianity, etc., and have translated the Epistles to the Hebrews and Galatians, with the Gospel by John. These I shall send home by the first opportunity, with my grammars of the Tahitian and of the Raratongan, which contain remarks on the New Zealand.

Naturally Williams did not confine his attentions to Rarotonga, but kept a close eye on the other Cook islands. This was only sensible, for he could carry out much more detailed supervision than could be accomplished by his colleagues on faraway Tahiti. Even so, some of his co-workers judged it a typical piece of Williams interference. On Rarotonga his activities included setting up trading ventures, abolishing polygamy, and building a bigger and better chapel. But he did not forget his first love — travelling. Before he had been on the island a year he was urging the Rarotongans to build him an eighty-ton sailing vessel for his missionary activities. Williams himself took a leading part in its building and it was completed in three months, yet another almost incredible achievement. It was called the *Messenger of Peace* and was the answer to his prayers, for now he had his own independent means of sailing about the South Pacific; it was all he asked for. A maiden voyage to Aitutaki was a resounding success and he returned to Rarotonga in a high good humour with a cargo of pigs, coconuts, and a number of cats to fight the menace of rats on the island. Having disembarked this cargo he decided with almost indecent haste that Charles Pitman and his wife were now ready to take over the mission, and so bidding them a fond but not protracted farewell he sailed for Raiatea where he spent the best part of a year lovingly strengthening the *Messenger of Peace* for the voyages that were to add fresh lustre to his name.

On 24 May 1830 John Williams and Brother John Barff, accompanied by seven native teachers, sailed from Raiatea. Their mission was to inspect those islands already converted and to spread the word to those not yet visited. One of their first stops was at Mangaia in the Cooks, where some native missionaries had converted a number of the islanders but had stirred up a civil war between the converts and the pagans. In this case the Christians seemed to have behaved with excessive zeal, slaughtering a number of their fellow-islanders. Williams was not happy about this but did his best to remedy the situation and continued on to Rarotonga and Aitutaki. Then he headed towards the north-west for the Friendly Islands.

At Tonga the Wesleyans were making steady progress but they welcomed the representatives of the LMS. At this stage there was no great jealousy between the different Protestant denominations working in the Pacific, for it was realised that there was more than enough work for all. It was at Tonga on this voyage that Williams came to an important agreement with the Wesleyans. On behalf of the London Missionary Society he agreed to allow them a free hand in the Friendly Islands if they in turn gave the LMS a clear run in Samoa, which was Williams's next destination. Altogether Williams and Barff spent two pleasant weeks with Turner and Cross of the Wesleyan Mission, and then set off for Samoa.

They reached the island in July and found it as yet largely unspoiled by contact with Europeans, because it was used as a watering place only by a few whalers. News of the missionaries had reached Samoa, however, brought by canoes blown off course or by islanders shipping as crew on European whalers. The people were willing to welcome both Williams and his message, especially since they seemed to be accompanied by brightly-coloured calico and iron tools. The chief of the district at which the *Messenger of Peace* had put in, Malietoa Vai'inupo, received them hospitably, even though he was engaged in a civil war at the time. Williams was impressed by the Samoans, and so was Brother Barff, who said that "a kind of careless contentment was depicted in all their countenances". Williams was quick to see that the island was ripe for conversion. There were no priests of any importance and therefore no vested interests with which to contend. News had also reached the islanders that on the whole, the missionaries had brought peace and a measure of prosperity to the districts in which they had so far settled. The "missionary kingdom" of Tahiti was well thought of by men of other islands who had visited it, and another aspect that gained favour with the Samoans was that the Christianity imposed by the LMS did not demand great changes in the way of life of its new adherents.

Greatly encouraged, Williams left some Polynesian teachers at Samoa and set sail once more. He decided that he had travelled enough for one voyage and headed back to Raiatea by way of Rarotonga, Mangaia, Tahiti and other islands. Reaching Raiatea he discovered that there had been a reaction to Christianity and that a number of the younger islanders had taken advantage of his absence to form a breakaway group. Responding to the challenge with a vengeance John Williams set to work to unite his divided island. It proved harder than he had anticipated: fighting broke out between the two factions and an attempt was made on the missionary's life. Williams gave the order for

The *Messenger of Peace* leaving Aitutaki. A wood engraving by G. Baxter in *A narrative of missionary enterprises in the South Sea Islands*, by John Williams, 1837.

firearms to be used if necessary and an extremely ugly situation developed with more than a little bloodshed before the affair was patched up by the intervention of some of the more influential chiefs from Tahiti. Altogether it was a distressing affair and a portent, though the missionaries did not know it, of the strong anti-Christian and anti-missionary drive that was to sweep the Society Islands in the near future.

When some order had been restored, Williams seized an opportunity to sail away in the *Messenger of Peace,* another action criticised by a number of his colleagues; but he had never made a secret of the fact that he regarded himself as a planter, not a cultivator. He headed for Rarotonga, hoping perhaps that the trouble in Raiatea would have blown over before his return. It was not to be. Rarotonga, now administered by Brother Buzacott, was having its own troubles, with the Christian converts fighting the unconverted. Williams did his best to help his colleagues, who were suffering from an outbreak of arson, but it was uphill work. Many islanders were coming to the conclusion that Christianity was more trouble than it was worth and that the missionaries were interfering too much in their lives.

During his attempts to placate the Rarotongans Williams saw the *Messenger of Peace* dashed on the shore in a storm, necessitating months of laborious repairs. Sadly he sailed for the Society Islands in the crippled vessel, but at Raiatea things were no better — in fact they were worse. To add to the troubles caused by the islanders' growing disenchantment with their new religion, traders had been selling rum and other spirits to the Raiateans, who had taken to this new vice with alacrity and were manufacturing their own alcohol. Williams's critics were later to claim that the missionary had been too much occupied with his voyaging and trading ventures to keep a close eye on his wayward parishioners. It is true that on his return on this occasion in 1831 the once all-powerful Williams found the greatest difficulty in controlling the Raiateans. This slackening of mission authority was being duplicated on the other islands of the Society group.

Williams did not exactly wash his hands of the Raiateans — to do so would be foreign to his persistent nature — but a certain perfunctory air is noticeable in his dealings with them after the monumental backsliding caused by the introduction of demon rum. The relatively undiscovered islands beyond the horizon seemed even more attractive to him and in October 1832 he sailed once more for Samoa. Here he discovered the mission to be operating satisfactorily. True, the Wesleyans had not left the island completely, according to their promise, but most of the Methodist outposts consisted of churches run by Tongan missionaries who perhaps did not understand the meaning of the agreement to divide the spheres of influence of the two Churches. There was another breakaway sect on Samoa, formed by a couple of castaway or runaway (opinions differed) sailors who had seen the perquisites in the shape of food and land grants and founded their own church.

These pinpricks aside, Williams had good cause to be pleased with what he found on Samoa. The islanders had taken joyfully to the externals of their new religion, singing the hymns with gusto, and the chief Malietoa had defeated his adversaries and embraced Christianity. At first he had been a little apprehensive and had hedged his bets, fearing that "the gods will be enraged with me for abandoning them and endeavour to destroy me? and perhaps Jehovah may not have power to protect me against the effects of their anger!". Accordingly Malietoa had proposed to adopt Christianity for a trial period and should nothing of an adverse nature occur his family and followers could then become converted in turn. The crucial period passed without event and Malietoa's followers joined him in the Christian camp.

Williams found that Malietoa had a great deal of influence and more than most island chiefs preferred to keep a restraining hand on the missionaries, requiring of them that they approach his people through him. As long as Malietoa maintained his supremacy this worked well enough for the LMS representatives, but it had its drawbacks. Some chiefs became jealous of Malietoa's monopoly of Christianity and a few years later one of them was to send to Tonga asking the Wesleyans to send some European missionaries to him so that his people too could adopt Christianity. His request was granted and Peter Turner was sent in 1834 before the authorities in the Methodist Church ordered him to withdraw because of the agreement to leave Samoa to the LMS.

In 1832 Williams was unaware of the awkwardness that was later to develop between the two Churches on Samoa. Well

The interior of Avarua chapel, Rarotonga. From *Gems From the Coral Islands, Volume II,* by the Rev. William Gill, Ward & Co, London, 1856.

satisfied with what he saw he left for Rarotonga, reaching there at the beginning of 1833. News of his voyages was now reaching Britain and catching the fancy of the public. Amid the general chorus of praise and admiration for his journeys in the *Messenger of Peace* was a message from the Archbishop of Canterbury who announced that by his missionary activities John Williams was adding a new chapter to the Acts of the Apostles.

At Rarotonga Williams found that Aaron Buzacott had everything well under control and that a religious revival was sweeping the island, a welcome change from the apathy and backslidings at Raiatea and Tahiti. So contrite for their sins were the natives that many of them brought back articles stolen from the missionaries over the past few years. Also, Buzacott had imported the printing press formerly belonging to William Ellis and was publishing books and pamphlets. He agreed eagerly to Williams's suggestion that a cloth-spinning industry be started and approved Williams's act of going to Tahiti and bringing back another European missionary to start a cotton factory.

Williams and his wife had been in the Pacific for almost seventeen years. Mrs Williams had suffered uncomplainingly in the heat and humidity and had watched a number of her children die. Now, in 1834, Williams decided it was time they went back to England for a break. While the ostensible reason for the journey was to allow his wife time to recover from her *malaise,* Williams had other reasons. There was his desire to publicise the work of the missionaries in the Pacific, to raise funds to enable the work to be continued, and to encourage young men to volunteer for service among the islands.

He spent four years in Britain, and from his point of view hardly a moment was wasted, for he stumped the country preaching and exhorting, everywhere being greeted by enthusiastic crowds; he supervised the printing of the New Testament in Rarotongan; he wrote and published *A Narrative of Missionary Enterprises in the South Sea Islands,* which sold 20,000 copies in the first three years and continued to sell steadily for several decades. He failed to persuade the Admiralty to grant him a naval vessel for his missionary voyages but it was a failure he could afford to shrug off when over £4,000 rolled in in donations, quite sufficient for the purchase of the stout 200-ton *Camden,* more than twice the size of the *Messenger of Peace,* which he had sold in the islands. He seemed to please everyone — the evangelists with his tales of missionary success, the merchants with his accounts of fortunes to be made by those who followed in the footsteps of the missions, the great public with his tales of derring-do.

On 11 April 1838 he sailed for the Pacific in the *Camden,* bearing with him the good wishes of hundreds of thousands whose imaginations had been fired by his stories and his example. It was the highlight of his life. The brief year remaining was to be one of disappointment culminating in his death.

On his return he found that in spite of the glowing reports still being returned to Britain by the LMS missionaries matters had gone from bad to worse. In the Society Islands and in other areas the islanders were turning away from Christianity, disillusioned and tired of the constant demands of the missionaries. The islanders were tired of working, tired of being forced into Mother Hubbards and other grotesque European clothing, tired of being forced to move their homes at the request of the missionaries so they could attend church services more often.

Epidemics were cutting down population in many islands, diseases introduced by the Europeans being responsible for many deaths.

Williams also discovered that the harmony hitherto existing between the different denominations was no longer so marked. The Methodists had entered Fiji and seemed to have claimed it for their own. The Catholics had gone into the South Pacific after a lapse of more than two hundred years. Williams gave vent to his feelings in a bitter letter:

> With regard to the Catholics, you will be grieved to hear that priests are making a most desperate effort to establish Popery in the islands. I have heard that a French frigate is gone to the Gambier Islands with fifty priests on board. What a call is this for exertion on the part of British Christians; and how ought the friends of Christ of all denominations to unite hand and heart in opposing that despicable and destructive system.

Williams moved away from Polynesia and towards the New Hebrides. He found the Melanesians a dour and suspicious assembly, each village a law unto itself with head-hunting and cannibalism rife. He also found that the atrocities committed by the sandalwood traders and other unscrupulous Europeans had made the inhabitants of the sultry New Hebrides even more withdrawn and apprehensive. Nevertheless Williams found himself oddly attracted by the area, mainly because of the challenge it presented. By November 1839 he was sailing in the *Camden* past the islands of the New Hebrides with a number of Samoan missionaries on board. In the four years he had been away, Samoa and Rarotonga had been the two main sources of hope for the LMS. Samoa in particular had proved particularly faithful to the Christian cause and there had been little trouble in attracting a dozen volunteers to serve in the savage New Hebrides. For years to come the native missionaries were to prove the main strength of Christian missions in the South Sea. They did remarkable work. Lacking the prestige of Europeans they were ignored, bullied and sometimes killed by the islanders with whom they cast in their lot, but almost to a man they persevered, and between 1839 and 1860 most faiths owed more than they cared to admit to these island missionaries who went where few Europeans dared to venture.

The massacre of the missionaries the Rev. John Williams and Mr Harris. An oil print by George Baxter, published in 1841. The print is held in the Alexander Turnbull Library, Wellington.

On 19 November Williams landed some Samoan teachers on Tanna where the islanders appeared to be tolerant. At this time he was seriously considering settling on one of the islands of the New Hebrides. It was also during this period that he wrote in his diary: "The approaching week is the most important of my life." The next day, 20 November, he landed at Erromanga, an island that had suffered cruelly at the hands of sandalwood traders eager to earn the £35-a-ton the wood was fetching in China, and where, according to one contemporary source, "it was well known that they (the inhabitants) had been often ill-treated by foreigners, and their shyness and distrust were attributed to that cause".

John Williams went ashore with Morgan, the captain of the *Camden,* and two other missionaries, Harris and Cunningham. They handed out gifts according to custom, and Williams and Harris walked along the beach in search of a drink of water. This changed the attitude of the islanders who had been reserved but not antagonistic. They had been preparing for a feast when the missionaries had landed and they were suddenly afraid that Williams and his companion would stumble across the feasting grounds and steal their food, as previous Europeans had done. Panic-stricken, some of the Erromangans surrounded the two missionaries. One of the leaders, Raniani, had seen his own son killed by visiting Europeans, and it seems he struck the first blow with a club.

The Europeans turned to run back to their boat. Cunningham and Captain Morgan, who had not ventured as far as the other two, reached it, but Harris fell while attempting to leap across a stream of water, and was killed with clubs and spears. Williams, too, stumbled, and was felled with a club. The Erromangans stood over him thrusting with their spears until he was dead. Then the natives dragged the two dead missionaries into the undergrowth and later ate them.

5

WE HAVE LONG BEEN WEEPING

The ten years following the death of John Williams on Erromanga witnessed a resurgence of missionary interest in the United Kingdom, a further slackening of the influence of the London Missionary Society, the remarkable efforts of native teachers among the islands, and the establishment of missions in the Pacific by the Roman Catholics, Presbyterians, and Anglicans.

The martyrdom of Williams, coming so soon after he had made such an impact in Britain with his speeches and writings, shocked many people. It received a great deal of publicity and led to a number of young men offering themselves as missionaries to the islands. Not all of these volunteers became members of the London Missionary Society; other religious organisations were beginning to take an interest in the South Seas and the sudden influx of enthusiasts did a certain amount towards strengthening the missionary ambitions of several denominations.

Meanwhile, on Tahiti the LMS missionaries were having a bad time. Since the death of Pomare II in 1821 they had been struggling, and the death six years later of the boy king Pomare III, in whom the missionaries had placed so much hope, was a further blow. By 1830, when Tahiti had become a popular port of call for the ever-increasing number of Pacific trading vessels, the missionaries were finding their task arduous in the extreme. They had particular difficulty with the sister of the late Pomare III, who became queen under the title of Pomare IV. She proved to have no interest in Christianity and distressed the missionaries beyond measure with her predilection for rum, adultery and dancing. To make matters worse, a former Tahitian deacon of the church, Teau, claimed to be Jesus Christ and led a breakaway religious movement.

Henry Nott and his colleagues did their best to combat the increasing drunkenness and prostitution and for a while had some success with temperance leagues and hastily-processed laws against various forms of immorality, but they were attempting to maintain a precarious dyke, and they themselves felt that at any moment the waters of sin would come pouring through. Not all the Tahitians were backsliders; some rallied to the support of the missionaries — but in a way this made matters even more desperate as it raised the threat of civil war. This came very close in 1830 when Pomare IV, offended at some slight real or imagined at the hands of the missionaries, went over to the breakaway *mamaia* sect. A British man-of-war arrived and acted as a temporary deterrent, but after it left fighting broke out between supporters of the queen and some of the minor chiefs, which ended in victory for Pomare IV's warriors.

The attitude of the Tahitians to the missionaries was no longer one of welcome or even tolerance. In 1839 one newly-arrived brother was driven to complain:

Whilst speaking about the stations on this island, I would at the same time make a few observations on the people, and I cannot but remark that their state is very different from what I expected and from the representations I have heard in England from the platform. Instead of giving me a kind and cordial reception, the people say my object and that of the new brethren is to trade and gain money. I find it almost impossible to eradicate from their minds this notion; they are continually requesting me to sell or give away my property, and in almost every dealing I have with them they attempt to defraud. Instead of finding them attached to their missionaries, I see them treat those gentlemen with disrespect and insolence. They subject them to innumerable petty annoyances and rob them frequently. Mr. Davies and Mr. Wilson have had property stolen repeatedly since my arrival, and Mr. Henry has been obliged to suspend his church lately for stealing his cattle; he thinks he has lost fifty head. They charge exorbitant prices for everything they sell or do, and insist on being paid in money; if we offer them cloth, they will not look at it, except it be of the gayest and best description; they prefer going to the stores of the merchants at Papeete for their goods. The prices they charge for tables and chairs here, and which after all are but clumsily made, are so high as to render it impossible to obtain them.

Pomare, Queen of Tahiti. An oil print by George Baxter, published in 1845. This print is held in the Alexander Turnbull Library Art Collection, Wellington.

The state of the churches here is very deplorable. I do not think I have met with one individual who is a member that does not evince the same covetousness exhibited by those who make no profession. The churches are large, and nearly all the chiefs and raatiras are members, but many of them are utterly unfit to sit down at the table of our Lord. The queen, a wicked and violent woman, is a member of a church, notwithstanding she late countenanced by her presence one of the native dances. Mr. Simpson has suspended his church on account of their return to the same heathen custom. . . .

It never rained but it poured: the missionaries, so long the undisputed rulers of the "missionary kingdom" of Tahiti now had to suffer the political interest of several Western nations. French vessels had begun to visit the area, and in 1834 a pearl trader from Belgium, Moerenhout, who had been in the Society

Islands before, returned from a visit to the USA with the news that he had been appointed United States Consul to Tahiti. The missionaries had long darkly suspected Moerenhout of being no friend of theirs and these suspicions were confirmed when, in 1836, two Roman Catholic priests visited Tahiti. Their arrival could hardly have caused more consternation among the agents of the London Missionary Society. Rumours of Catholic infiltration had been spreading, and indeed for some time it had been known that the Catholics had been on the Mangareva group since 1834.

The two priests — Fathers Laval and Caret — had in fact come to Tahiti from the Mangarevas. They were given permission to remain on the island by a number of the chiefs and were offered hospitality by Moerenhout. They approached the queen and asked her permission to live and work on Tahiti, but the LMS missionaries had reached the queen first and Pomare IV ordered the immediate deportation of the two priests. Some of her subjects reacted a little too enthusiastically to their monarch's commands, besieged the Catholics in Moerenhout's house and hustled the two rather frightened men on to the first departing vessel, which happened to be going to Wallis Island, where the priests were deposited. But Tahiti had not heard the last of them or their colleagues.

The missionary who had led the outcry against them was George Pritchard, a Birmingham man who by this time was beginning to take the place of the aging Nott as the leader of the missionaries on Tahiti. Born like John Williams, in 1796, the year of the pioneering voyage of the *Duff* on behalf of the London Missionary Society, Pritchard was the son of working-class parents and served a trade apprenticeship, ending up as a brassfounder. By the time he was eighteen Pritchard was serving as a preacher for the Congregationalist Church, and by his determination and eloquence attracted the interest of some of the LMS representatives who were constantly on the lookout for potential missionaries. He liked the idea of serving in the Pacific islands and applied for consideration as a missionary, but the leaders of the LMS were by no means impressed by the young man's elementary education. Pritchard himself confessed: "As I have been employed at a trade ever since I was young, my advantages of education or subsequent improvement have been very scanty. I have nearly gone through the English Grammar, I have learnt a system of shorthand, and I have attended some little to Geography."

In spite of an initial lukewarm report, Pritchard was still marked down as a young man to be watched, and he was placed under a Stafford clergyman for a year as a combined student and assistant. Pritchard proved to have great energy and a retentive memory. From Stafford he went for four years to the LMS theological college conducted at Gosport by the Reverend Dr Bogue. In 1824 he was accepted as a candidate for missionary work in the Pacific, and was ordained a few weeks later. On 14 December he and his young wife arrived at Tahiti.

Overshadowed by such personalities as Henry Nott, John Williams, and William Ellis, George Pritchard laboured quietly and conscientiously for many years in the Society Islands, seeing in the process the gradual deterioration of the prestige and effectiveness of the LMS missionaries in the area. A contemporary of Pritchard on Tahiti for a while was Melville, later to write *Moby Dick* and *Billy Budd*. Melville wrote several books about the South Seas, one of them, *Omoo,* dealing with his time in the Society Islands. While paying perfunctory compliments to the achievements of the missionaries — banning idolatory, establishing schools, and introducing literacy — Melville was not impressed with the LMS, writing:

Doubtless in thus denationalising the Tahitians, as it were, the missionaries were prompted by a sincere desire for good; but the effect has been lamentable. Supplied with no amusements in place of those forbidden, the Tahitians, who require more recreation than other people, have sunk into a listlessness, or indulge in sensualities, a hundred times more pernicious than all the games ever celebrated in the Temple of Tanee.

Pritchard would have paid little attention to such criticisms. As time went on the Birmingham missionary became more and more self-assured. Other missionaries retired or gave up, but Pritchard persevered, working quietly and consistently. In addition to his mission work he engaged in trading activities, as did many of his colleagues, and did very well out of them. He also gained the attention of the queen. Pritchard's mission work was centred on the port of Papeete where he was able to see the queen regularly and also to keep himself informed of what was going on by interviewing the captains of visiting vessels. With his trading ventures flourishing he was able to live well and entertain in style. He became self-confident and, some said, arrogant. Queen Pomare, married for a second time and disinclined for any more fighting in her realm, began to lean increasingly on the handsome and energetic Pritchard for advice and guidance. In 1832 she suggested in a letter to England that George Pritchard be made British Consul-general at Tahiti. There were those unkind enough to suggest that the letter had been written at the missionary's instigation.

The first request for the appointment of Pritchard was not granted. In 1836, however, a second request was made. By this time the situation had changed: Moerenhout, a former friend of Pritchard but now anything but an ally, had been made American Consul, and the thought of a Belgian Roman Catholic as a United States representative in Tahiti was disturbing to Lord Melbourne in London. A number of British residents, Queen Pomare herself and Rear-Admiral Sir George Hammond, British Naval Commander-in-Chief in the Pacific, all gave their support to Pritchard's claim, and in 1838 it was agreed to. The missionary had become a diplomat.

Needless to say, George Pritchard's political activities did not find favour with many of his colleagues both in Tahiti and at the headquarters of the London Missionary Society. Letters travelled laboriously to and from London and Tahiti. Pritchard was reproached by colleagues and superiors. He remained adamant; he saw nothing irreconcilable in his twin functions as missionary and Consul-general. He would give up neither post.

His appointment became anything but a sinecure. The Roman Catholic priests ejected from Tahiti had complained to the French Government that they, French citizens, had been badly treated in the Society Islands. (Father Caret, a man of some persistence, had tried a second time to land at Tahiti in 1837 and had been sent packing almost as summarily as the first occasion.) The French sent the *Venus,* captained by Dupetit-Thouars, to the Pacific. The captain deposited two Roman Catholic priests in the Marquesas, then went on to Tahiti, where he trained the guns of his frigate on Papeete and intimated that the French authorities

George Pritchard, "her Britannic Majesty's Consul" in Tahiti. An oil print by George Baxter, published in 1845. This print is in the Alexander Turnbull Library Art Collection, Wellington.

would not be averse to collecting the sum of 2,000 Spanish dollars. This, announced Dupetit-Thouars blandly, was the fine imposed by the French Government for the ill-treatment of the priests who had been banished from Tahiti. The letter the captain sent to the queen left her in no doubt of his intentions:

Madam,

The King and Government of France, justly angered by the outrage done to their nation by the wrong and ignoble treatment meted out to several of their nationals who have landed on Tahitian soil, and, in particular, in 1836 to MM. Laval and Caret, Apostolic Missionaries, have sent me to demand, and if necessary enforce, the prompt reparations due to a powerful Nation that has been gravely and unprovokedly insulted.

The King and his Government demand:

1. That the Queen of Tahiti write to the King of France to apologize for the violence and other insults committed against Frenchmen whose honourable conduct did not

deserve the punishment inflicted on them. The Queen's letter shall be written in Polynesian and in French and the two texts shall be signed by her. This letter shall be officially delivered to the Commandant of the *Venus* within twenty-four hours of the present notification:

2. That the sum of 2,000 Spanish dollars shall be paid into the Coffers of the Frigate *Venus* within twenty-four hours, following the present notification, as an indemnity to MM. Laval and Caret, as damages for the acts committed against them:

3. That the Flag of France be flown at noon on 1 September on the island of Motu-Otu and receive a salute of twenty-one guns from the Queen's fortress.

I declare to Your Majesty that in default of the satisfaction demanded being received within the prescribed time, I shall find myself very regretfully obliged to declare and to commence hostilities against the States under your dominion and that such hostilities will be continued by all ships of war that will successively visit these Islands until France has received satisfactory reparations.

I am with profound respect Your Majesty's very humble servant.

The Commandant of the Frigate *Venus*

(Sgd.) A. Dupetit-Thouars.

Horrified and embittered, Queen Pomare sent an immediate letter of apology. There was then a short and vitriolic interview with the unfortunate George Pritchard, whose advice had put her in this untenable position. Fiercely she upbraided the hapless British Consul-general, informing him that she could not and would not find the 2,000 Spanish dollars demanded by France. Pritchard recognised an ultimatum when he heard one: hastily he provided 500 of the required dollars himself and raised the remainder in loans. He even went out to the *Venus* and sheepishly borrowed enough powder from the French captain to enable Queen Pomare to fire the required twenty-one-gun salute. It was a bad time for the missionary and was made no better by the knowledge that Moerenhout was lurking about, enjoying every moment. The Belgian, thanks to some vigorous intriguing on the part of Pritchard, had been dismissed and replaced by the

Americans as their local representative. Dupetit-Thouars had fetched with him from France more than threats of reprisals; he had brought the news that Moerenhout was now to be the *French* representative on Tahiti.

For Queen Pomare, twenty-eight years old and salad days behind her, bearing the afflictions heaped upon her with dignity, it was just one more blow. To Pritchard and the LMS missionaries it was disaster. A Roman Catholic, backed by the armed might of France, had an official position on Tahiti. It could only be the start of a new era.

The Catholics had not been in the Pacific in any force since Quiros gave up his attempt to found New Jerusalem in the New Hebrides at the beginning of the seventeenth century. Two hundred years later they began to return, at first in small parties venturing from Peru — one attempt at Matavai in the Society Islands failed in 1775. Catholic explorers of the calibre of Dumont d'Urville and Peter Dillon had urged the Catholic authorities to send missionaries to the area, and serious consideration began to be given to the matter by about 1822. A political tinge was given when it was recognised that most Protestant missionaries in the Pacific were British, while the Catholics who were beginning to arrive were mainly French. In 1825 Roman Catholics landed at Hawaii. These priests from the Society of Pipcus, or the Congregation du Sacre-Coeur de Jesus et de Marie, found the American Board of Missions representatives too well entrenched to make much progress and were expelled from the islands. Not long afterwards the Pope granted the newly-founded vicariate of Eastern Oceania to the Society of Pipcus. The Pacific islands were given into the charge of Mgr Etienne Rouchouse who was declared Bishop of Nilopolis. On 7 August 1834 Fathers Caret and Laval and Brother Murphy landed in the Mangareva (Gambier) group of islands. They survived a dangerous opening period when they were attacked by the islanders, but a knowledge of medicine among the fathers proved propitious, for they were able to save the stricken son of one of the chiefs. Many of the islanders were converted and when Bishop Rouchouse arrived in 1835 with more missionaries most of the people had embraced Catholicism.

Encouraged by this success the Bishop sent Brother Murphy

to Tahiti to see whether the Catholics could form a mission there as well. Brother Murphy posed as a ship's carpenter, but was soon detected by George Pritchard, who sent him packing. His visit was followed by the abortive attempt of Fathers Caret and Laval, which in turn led to the arrival of the *Venus* and the payment by Pritchard of the indemnity of 2,000 Spanish dollars.

Now the Catholics were beginning to enter the Pacific in some force. Much of the strength of the Catholic missions came from France where there was a considerable revival of the faith following the Napoleonic wars. In 1822 Pauline Jaricot formed the Ouevre de la Propagation de la Foi, an organisation which collected funds to support Catholic missions overseas. Another source of support was the Société de l'Oceanie, formed in 1845 by Victor Marziou, and it was intended to finance trading ventures in the Pacific and at the same time provide free passages for Catholic missionaries working there.

With the Pipcus brothers beginning to gain a foothold in Polynesia the Papal "Ministry of Missions" (the Sacred Congregation for the Propagation of the Faith), began to turn its thoughts to sending missionaries to the western Pacific. This task was given to the Marists, or Société de Marie, under the leadership of Jean-Claude Colin who was declared Superior General of the order in 1836. In the same year Bishop Jean Baptiste Pompallier took the first band of Marist missionaries to the Pacific, his vicariate consisting of all the Pacific islands west of the Cooks. Pompallier left missionaries on the islands of Wallis and Futuna and went on to make his headquarters in New Zealand.

The first two missionaries who had been landed on the islands had mixed fortunes. Father Bataillon on Wallis converted all the islanders in four years. He spent forty years there becoming the first Vicar Apostolic of Central Oceania. His colleague Father Chanel was martyred on Futuna on 28 April 1841.

Other Catholic priests had landed at Tonga in 1839 and again in 1841, but each time had been refused permission to stay by the leader Taufa'ahau who explained that his people were already Christians and had no need of new faiths. In 1842 the Catholics gained a foothold in the pagan district of Bea, where they converted many of the islanders. Thousands of miles to the north-

The Venerable John Claud Colin (1790-1875). Frontispiece to the *Venerable John Claud Colin*, by Georges Goyali, Dublin.

east, at Hawaii, the Catholics had been less successful. In 1836 one priest, Father Walsh, had been allowed to stay, but when he was joined the following year by Fathers Bachelot and Short, Hiram Bingham and the other American Board of Missions representatives sent up a howl of protest. King Kamehameha III ordered the priests to leave Honolulu. Objections were made, notably by the captain of the British man-of-war *Sulphur* and by the ubiquitous Dupetit-Thouars who was on his way to humiliate George Pritchard and Queen Pomare at Tahiti; but the king was adamant, and the priests were forced to leave.

The Catholics worked on, meeting both success and failure. Pritchard had appealed for British protection in Tahiti and the Foreign Office gave judicial consideration to his claim, but while they were deliberating France sent a vessel to Tahiti and then on to Hawaii to ensure that both territories admitted Roman Catholics and allowed freedom of worship. The declaration signed by Queen Pomare and her chiefs in Tahiti went in part:

> The free exercise of the Catholic religion is to be permitted in the island of Tahiti and in all other possessions of Queen Pomare. The French Catholics there shall enjoy all the privileges accorded to the Protestants, without, however, being allowed under any pretext to meddle in the religious affairs of the country.

When Moerenhout suggested in 1840 that France, to compensate for the British occupation of New Zealand, should annexe Tahiti, it was the last straw as far as the British Consul-general was concerned. Pritchard hurriedly left for Britain, hoping to lay his claim before Queen Victoria and her ministers. In his absence Moerenhout, backed by the ever-present Dupetit-Thouars, declared a French protectorate over Tahiti. Queen Pomare, who had been holidaying in the Leeward Islands while most of Moerenhout's negotiations with some of her chiefs took place, hurried back to Papeete to find the island in turmoil. The confusion increased when it appeared that Dupetit-Thouars and Moerenhout had acted on their own initiative, and that the French Government knew nothing of Tahiti being made a French protectorate.

Moerenhout had gone too far to withdraw. Despite his ill-health — he had been savagely attacked and almost crippled by a sneak-thief some years before, and increasing trouble with some of the Catholic priests landing at Tahiti (Moerenhout felt they were too demanding over land rights) — he stubbornly continued to press for a French protectorate over the Society Islands. In Britain Pritchard could get little sense from Lord Aberdeen at the Foreign Office and returned to Tahiti, bearing as some consolation a carriage and a golden crown as presents for Queen Pomare.

The situation was now chaotic. Moerenhout, backed by Dupetit-Thouars, confronted Pritchard, who was reinforced by Captain Toup Nicolas, a jingoistic officer commanding HMS *Vindictive*. Queen Pomare must have felt like a bone being snarled over by a pack of angry dogs. The distracted queen even addressed a pathetic letter to her fellow-monarch, Queen Victoria:

Still continue to assist me, beloved Queen. This is my request to you, devise means by which peace may be restored to my Kingdom.

This is my desire, that the King of France would remove the individual J. A. Moerenhout, the French Consul. This man, by money and other bribes has turned away the hearts of my chief People from their Sovereign, so that they have become traitors to their Queen. This Man will not regard the Laws of my Land, but his own will he alone regards, and his general conduct brings to light his evil character. . . .

All the action seemed to be taking place on Tahiti. In London the Queen's advisers were against Britain becoming embroiled with

France at such a distance, especially as Her Majesty's Government tacitly recognised the right of France to annexe Tahiti and the Marquesas, since Britain had recently taken possession of New Zealand. On the spot, however, Pritchard and Moerenhout continued to be at daggers drawn, to the annoyance and chagrin of their respective governments. France ratified the protection treaty presented by Dupetit-Thouars; Pritchard encouraged Pomare IV to fly a specially-designed flag bearing a crown; Dupetit-Thouars demanded that the flag be lowered; Pomare refused; The French sent 500 men ashore, hauled down the flag, deposed the queen and declared that Tahiti was now a French protectorate. It was 7 November 1843.

It was the signal for more dissension. Pomare appealed to her people to keep calm and not to attempt to attack the French. The missionaries and businessmen on the island begged Pritchard to add his weight to maintaining peace. A French sailor was beaten up. The French declared that Pritchard had encouraged or condoned the attack. Pritchard was forcibly arrested and thrown into a dungeon. A few days later he was transferred to a French frigate and then to a British vessel which carried him back to England. Much more was to happen on Tahiti, but certainly the "missionary kingdom" there had come to an end.

Though the French Catholics had cause to be satisfied with what was happening on Tahiti, in other areas of the Pacific they had less reason for pleasure. There had been some strife within the Church itself. Dissension had begun when Jean-Claude Colin, the Superior General of the Marist Order, had become dissatisfied with Bishop Pompallier who was in charge of the Marists in the Pacific. Colin felt that the Bishop had been less than efficient and that some of the Marists in the South Sea were starving and badly administered. In an effort to maintain a Marist stronghold in the Pacific, the Superior General suggested that a series of separate vicariates be set up. In his turn Pompallier refused to allow any more Marist missionaries to join his force in the Pacific islands. He was particularly offended by the action of one priest, Jean-Baptiste Epalle, who returned to Europe from New Zealand in 1842, criticising Pompallier's actions. Epalle and Colin got together and presented to the Church authorities in

Bishop Jean-Baptiste Epalle, SM, 1811-1845.

Rome a scheme for missionary activity in Melanesia and Micronesia, pointing out with truth that apart from a few isolated traders these areas had not so far been corrupted by Europeans. The Marists also noted that it could only be a matter of time before the ever-growing number of white men in the Pacific spilled over from Polynesia to the Melanesian islands farther west.

This document was considered and approved by Cardinal Fransoni and others in authority in Rome. In 1844 permission was given for the formation of the vicariates of Micronesia and Melanesia, with Epalle consecrated as the Bishop in charge. Enthusiastically Epalle urged the need for speed in departing for the Pacific, and outlined his suggestions for the deployment of his missionaries, saying that it was in the interests of the Church:

> . . . as smartly as possible to possess ourselves of the principal groups and to send *quam primum* three or four priests and as many brothers to the Solomon Islands where there are seven islands, the least of which is almost as valuable as Tahiti . . . three or four priests and as many brothers for New Ireland and New Britain, each of which could be a diocese; three or four priests and as many brothers on each of the four or five principal points of New Guinea . . . if once the Europeans penetrate these islands the conversion of their inhabitants will present difficult obstacles; since we will have not only to combat infidelity but heresy and unbelief.

On 2 February 1845 Epalle, together with seven priests and six brothers, sailed from London and reached Sydney on 22 June. Here the Bishop did his best to find out what he could about Melanesia, but there was little to be discovered. Mendana had occupied parts of the Solomons for a few months almost three hundred years before; John Williams had been killed in the New Hebrides only six years ago; a few explorers and traders had put in at various islands. What reports there were seemed hardly encouraging. The Melanesians, more dour than the extrovert Polynesians, were savage fighters, jealous of their land rights, suspicious of strangers and given to head-hunting and cannibalism; other than this little else was known about them or their islands.

Bishop Epalle decided that his first expedition would be to the Solomon Islands, among the farthest west and most isolated of all the islands of the South Pacific. There were written descriptions of good landing places on San Cristobal and Santa Ysabel, and Epalle decided in the first instance to make for Makira Bay on the former island and then go on to Thousand Ships Bay. The Marists reached San Cristobal in December, where they found the islanders eager to trade, and ten days later sailed on to Astrolabe Harbour in Thousand Ships Bay.

On Santa Ysabel they were greeted in a friendly fashion but warned to proceed no farther as the people beyond Maunga Point at the mouth of the harbour were enemies of the people Epalle was talking to. He dismissed this warning as an exaggeration and on 16 December led a party towards the so-called dangerous territory. Father Chaurain, a member of the expedition, later gave this account of what happened:

> . . . the natives came out in 60 canoes; they swarmed round the ship. We landed and saw before us a sort of army of natives, drawn up on the sand. Some seemed frightened and withdrew behind the trees; 50 or 60 others stood their ground. We made signs to them, an old man with white hair and beard came trembling towards the boat, with a spear and a shield in his hands. He gave us some fruit as a present, and we gave him a small piece of iron. Bishop Epalle, Brother Prosper and I went ashore with the mate and two sailors, two other sailors guarding the boat; their arms were left behind in the boat.
>
> The old man returned to the crowd and gave the iron to a

young man of about 25, tall, well-made and fair, armed with a richly ornamented shield and spear, and tomahawk, evidently their chief. He received it with contempt. The mate brought him to the boat, and gave him a small axe, which he carried back proudly, holding it aloft. . . .

Fr. Fremont asked where the houses were, but there was no answer. Several chiefs were pointed out. We complimented a chief on his fine tomahawk, but we only received a proud look. A young man offered two lemons, one partly eaten, for the Bishop's ring. We saw a European axe in the hands of one of them, and I pointed out another to the Bishop. They began to threaten us and P. said "They seem to be ready for a fight." The Bishop agreed and said it was a pity the sailors had not brought their arms. He took a few steps towards the boat, but was already surrounded by a dozen natives.

We saw the Bishop struck on the head from behind by a native of very short stature, and they set up a horrible war-whoop. The Bishop cried out in pain and put both hands to his head. Now the attack became general, each of the natives selected his own victim. Each of us saw several tomahawks raised over his head, and all ran. P. saw the Bishop receive another blow from an axe. . . .

Two hours after the party had left on its fatal expedition it returned, carrying Epalle. He died three days later and was buried on the island of San Jorge. Father Fremont assumed command and took the missionaries back to the safety of Makira Bay, where the Marists were at first welcomed and even allowed to buy land. The mission was not a success. During the next two years three of the missionaries were killed and another died. The priests and brothers finally abandoned the mission in 1852. Another mission was started in the same year on Tikopia, a Polynesian island in the Eastern Solomons, but a year later when a vessel put in to visit them the priests had vanished.

Though the London Missionary Society was fast losing ground on Tahiti, its training schools at Rarotonga and Samoa were preparing islanders to travel the South Seas as Christian missionaries. In Rarotonga the Rev. Aaron Buzacott was the guiding light, training his charges in a knowledge both of the Scriptures

The death of Bishop Epalle. An illustration from *In the savage South Solomons*, by the Right Rev. L. M. Raucaz, 1928.

and carpentry. For almost thirty years he ran his college in the Cook Islands, sending many native missionaries to the other islands of the Pacific. They were responsible for something of a religious revival in the 1840s.

The New Hebrides, the scene of the death of John Williams, saw many of these teachers. Indeed, until the Presbyterian Churches in Scotland and the Dominions started to send white missionaries to the area towards the end of the decade, the Samoans and Rarotongans were the only Christian missionaries in this part of the Pacific.

The area had of course been opened up by John Williams shortly before his martyrdom. Only two days before he had described an encounter with some of the New Hebrideans:

We began to doubt whether or not the island was inhabited; but on nearing the coast, we discovered cultivated soil and little low huts. Two canoes came off to us, in one of which were four men; their faces were thickly besmeared with a red pigment, and a long feather was stuck in the hair, at the back of the head; and various ornaments of tortoiseshell rings were suspended from the lobes of each ear ,and from the cartilage of the nose.

It was at this island, Futuna, that two Samoan teachers, Samson and Abela, were landed in 1841. They spent three years preaching and teaching on the island with their wives, but in 1845 an epidemic struck and the islanders blamed the "sacred men" and killed them and their wives and children. Some years later the Anglican Bishop of New Zealand, Bishop Selwyn, landed and took away with him two youths for training in New Zealand. He returned them in 1852, writing:

Today we landed our two Fortuna scholars, and left them in the hands of their relatives, with our prayers and blessing, but with great uncertainty as to their future progress, as there are no teachers now on the island. This is one of the islands in which the London Missionary Society has obtained a vested interest, by the death of two of its teachers. . . .

If the death or injury of its teachers were to be held as the criterion of interest in a place then the LMS was to have many such claims to a monopoly in Melanesia in the middle of the nineteenth century. In 1841 the Rev. A. W. Murray landed two native teachers on New Caledonia. It was two years before the mission ship returned with more teachers, to find that one of the original men had died within weeks of being landed; the other had survived somehow. The mission ship left for another two years. One of the teachers left behind wrote:

We have joy; for the word of God is growing in this land of New Caledonia. Many of the people have learnt to read, and are attentive to worship every Sabbath-day. A few days ago a heathen came to me to enquire about casting away his idols. I told him an idol is nothing at all; that Jehovah is the true God; that he made the heavens, the earth and all things; that He has pitied us in our sins and death, and had sent his son Jesus to be our saviour.

Unfortunately the missionaries had little success on New Caledonia, and the weeping teachers were taken away on the next mission boat. Soon after they left there was internecine strife on the islands of the group and most of the natives who had been converted were slaughtered. Then the sandalwood traders descended, corrupting the islanders where they did not attack them, and when a mission ship returned with more teachers some years later it was to discover that the former mission station had been razed to the ground. It was not until the French and the Marists took an interest in New Caledonia that Christianity really took hold. The LMS tried hard there, especially on the Isle of Pines, an island well known in the Pacific. It had been visited by Polynesians, especially Tongan traders, for hundreds of years before it was sighted and named by Cook.

Captain Samuel Henry, the Tahitian-born son of an LMS missionary, put in at the island several times between 1828 and 1830. On one visit he encountered a group of Tongans and one Samoan whose canoe had been wrecked on the shores of the island. These Polynesians declared that the natives were anxious to receive missionaries. In 1840 two Samoan teachers were landed, and when the chief Touru was asked for an assurance of their safety he was highly offended and the Rev. A. W. Murray left convinced that the Samoans would be well looked after. When he returned a year later, however, it was to discover that Touru had been so flattered and praised by sandalwood traders that, in the words of one of the missionaries, "his attention and that of his people were entirely diverted from religion to matters far more congenial to the human heart". Touru objected to the Christian teachers standing up in his presence to preach the word of God, and scolded and struck them. When an epidemic, probably brought to the island by traders, swept the island the chief blamed the Samoan missionaries. Fortunately they were taken off by a visiting ship, lucky to escape with their lives.

The crew of one of the ships taking missionaries to the Isle of Pines took samples of sandalwood back to Australia and many ships were fitted out to swoop on the island. The hitherto quiet place became a centre of the trade. One skipper who had lived in Samoa claimed to be a missionary and hastily filled his ship with the wood before sailing away. Thus the missionaries became associated in the minds of the islanders with this trade, and when the excesses of the traders became abhorrent they exacted revenge on the Samoans. On one occasion the enraged islanders massacred the crew of a trading ship and also killed three Christian teachers. In 1852 when Bishop Selwyn of New Zealand visited the island the sandalwood trade was virtually ended and he found things much quieter. When the French and the Marists took over the group the worst punitive actions of the islanders had ended.

On Tanna in the New Hebrides, later to be famed for the work of John Geddie of the Presbyterian Church, the LMS also landed native teachers. The first missionary visit to the island had been by John Williams the day before his death.

"When will you come back?" they had asked him as he left.

In 1842 two missionaries, Brothers Turner and Nisbet, did land. Before long an epidemic broke out. Almost alone on the island the missionaries were unaffected, but they were blamed for the disease and hundreds of islanders advanced on the mission house. The two missionaries and their wives put to sea, followed by some Samoan teachers who had accompanied them. A contrary wind drove all back on to the beach, and they were about to be killed by the furious populace when an Australian vessel, *Highlander*, appeared and took the Christians on board and carried them to Samoa and safety.

Two years later the missionary vessel *John Williams* took Samoan and Rarotongan teachers to Tanna. No European missionaries accompanied them. It is difficult to avoid the impression that at this time some of the European missionaries were rather like a prizefighter's second, urging their principal into the ring while they stayed safely outside the arena. At first the islanders welcomed the missionaries, but soon changed their minds and killed several. Again the survivors fled on a providential trading vessel only, with great courage, to return later. In 1850 one of them, Tumataiapo, soon to die so far from home, was to write to the parent Church at Rarotonga:

My brethren, blessings on you all from our Lord Jesus, the Messiah. I and my companions are still alive on Tana. We are continuing to do the work of Jesus in this dark land. Our hearts are often crying because of the wickedness of the people of this land, but we are not quite destitute of joy. Our work is a work of joy; and Jesus is fulfilling his work. "Lo, I am with you even to the end of the world." The work is growing here. We want more brethren to help us. I am now very ill. I cannot say what will befall me, whether I am to live or die. Oh, pray for Tana, and send us more help.

Help was forthcoming. From Rarotonga and Samoa the teachers continued to come to the Melanesian islands. They landed and they worked and they prayed, and they wrote back

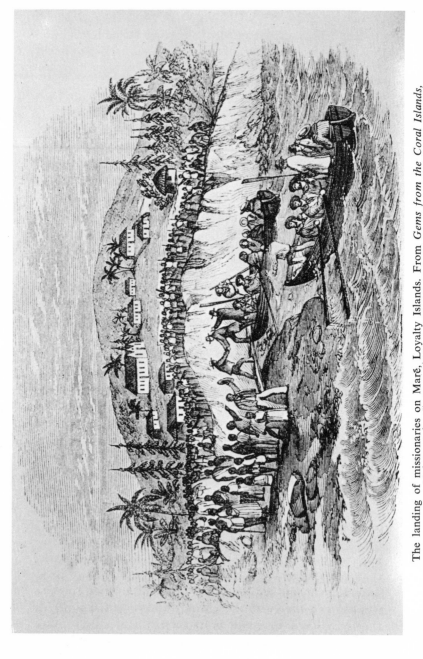

The landing of missionaries on Maré, Loyalty Islands. From *Gems from the Coral Islands, Volume I*, by the Rev. William Gill, Ward & Co., London, 1856.

to the Church at Rarotonga. Their letters present a picture of their efforts, their hopes and aspirations. From Maré, after three years on the island, some of them wrote in 1847:

We have long been weeping, but now we are becoming glad. We see our work is not altogether in vain. Our house is open for daily teaching. Many of the old folk frequently come, and are attentive to instruction; and nearly all the children who live near us are constant in their attendance. We have week-day services for explaining the work of God, and two public assemblies for worship on the Sabbath. These are now well attended; but, alas! the poor people come, almost without exception, in their heathen, naked condition. Some few of them get plaited leaves, which they wear around the loins; but, alas! as we look at them, our heart is sick with compassion towards them, and we have already given to them all the native cloth sent by you last year.

It was a story repeated in many places. The Melanesian islands, the New Hebrides, New Caledonia, the Solomons, the Isle of Pines, had mainly been left alone by the Polynesians who feared and distrusted the surly, quick-tempered cannibals of the Western Pacific. Europeans, too, had been slow to visit the humid Melanesian islands until driven there by the lust for a quick profit to be made out of sandalwood, and even then the traders left as quickly as they could. Not so the native teachers; they stayed on an island for life if they were allowed to do so. In spite of the fever and disease and the intense parochialism of the small tribal units, the Rarotongans and Samoans did their best to settle and remain.

The first native teachers landed on Aneityum in 1841. For six years they persevered until they were joined by European missionaries, but even then their troubles were not ended. A party of native teachers driven from neighbouring Tanna fled to Aneityum, where the anti-Christian element took heart from the fact that the Christians had been banished from Tanna and redoubled their efforts to dismiss them from Aneityum as well. They drove the missionaries from their settlements to a barren inland area where they almost died.

On Efaté the islanders had been terrorised by a band of Maoris who had mutinied and killed their captain when their ship had put

"Natives of Aneiteum carrying timber to build a church." From *Missions in Western Polynesia*, by A. W. Murray, John Snow, London/G. R. Addison, Sydney, 1863.

in to the island. Eight of the Maoris died of disease and two
more managed to escape on a trading ship, but when four Samoan
teachers landed on Efaté in 1845 they were taken for Maoris and
almost killed. They managed to survive for eighteen months, and
their joy at the return of the *John Williams* is described by a
chronicler of the London Missionary Society:

> The unbounded joy of these faithful men at again seeing the
> ship, after eighteen months' residence among such savage
> cannibals as the people of Faté, and in much suspense as to
> the vessel's return, can better be imagined than written. In the
> embrace of their native Christian brethren, they fell prostrate on
> the deck; sobs and cries for some time gave relief to the joy
> of their overflowing hearts, ànd as soon as they could speak,
> words of praise were the first sound we heard. "Faafetai i le
> Atua! Faafetai i le Atua i tona alofa tele!" Praise be to God!
> Praise be to God for His great love.

The rejoicing was premature. The mission ship sailed away and
it was two years before it returned, this time to a scene of
desolation. Some of the Samoans had died of different diseases,
and one had been ill and delirious. It was the custom of the people
of Efaté to kill any man "possessed of evil spirits", and accordingly
a crowd of men advanced on the house of the stricken teacher.
The Samoan managed to stagger from his bed and pile a barricade
of boxes against the door but the crowd broke in and killed him.

For years Efaté remained dangerous for missionaries. In 1854
two Rarotongans, Pikikaa and Kaveriri, together with their wives
were murdered, and as late as 1856 the LMS was saying of the
island "Efaté is at present under a cloud — this is the hour of the
powers of darkness there."

The darkness eventually lifted — in other islands as well as
Efaté — but the fact that it did so owed much to the efforts of the
Samoan and Rarotongan teachers who, almost alone, kept
Christianity in the Pacific for these vital years of the nineteenth
century.

6

WHERE NO SABBATH SMILES

By the middle of the nineteenth century, Christianity had been introduced by missionaries of one sort or another and with varying degrees of success to most of the islands of the Pacific. In some areas the new religion had been accepted by the majority of islanders, their reasons for embracing it differing considerably. For some it was a matter of economics and self-interest. As one Samoan chief explained in 1842:

It is my wish that the Christian religion should become universal among us. I look at the wisdom of these worshippers of Jehovah and see how superior they are to us in every respect. Their ships are like floating houses, so that they can traverse the tempest-driven ocean for months with safety, whereas if a breeze blow upon our canoes, they are in an instant upset and we are thrown into the sea. Their persons are covered from head to foot in beautiful clothes, while we have nothing but a girdle of leaves. The God who has given his white worshippers these great things must be wiser than our gods, for they have not given the like to us. We want all these articles, and my proposition is that the God who gave them should be our God.

It was this feeling that perhaps the Christian religion — *lotu* as it was known in many islands — might be more effective against misfortune than their pagan faith and should at least be given a trial, that was responsible for the introduction of Christianity in some areas. Sometimes the new faith proved ineffective, or the need for it died away. Ian Hogbin records that as late as 1912 in the Longgu area of Guadalcanal, islanders were distressed when an epidemic of dysentery swept the district. The elders attributed the visitation to the displeasure of the spirit Luvu because a dog had taken a bone into his shrine and the islanders had not expiated the sacrilege with sufficient offerings. The people, feeling that the god was being unduly spiteful, sent to the Anglican mission on another island and asked that a native teacher come and explain Christianity. By the time the teacher arrived the epidemic was over and the islanders no longer had need of a stronger *mana,* so after hanging around dismally for a few months the catechist was about to be sent back to his mission station. A neighbouring family invited him to remain with them, however, and so the white man's religion gained a foothold in the area.

Christianity was regarded by some as a symbol of prestige, being allied with the Europeans and the more educated among the islanders. With some missions the Christian *taboos* were less onerous than those imposed by pagan faiths and therefore worthy of adoption. The more thoughtful of the island chiefs also allied themselves with the missions against the less attractive Europeans who preyed upon them, securing for themselves the coveted firearms which the missionaries were sometimes prepared to dole out if they thought the islanders' cause just or expedient. In many cases islanders merely adopted some of the items of the Christian faith, mingling them with their pagan beliefs in the hope that they would get the best of both worlds.

Thousands 'of islanders, however, became genuine converts, especially in areas where the missionaries were men of patience, able to adapt their teaching to local conditions and capable of showing in their own lives that they were true Christians. The Rarotongans and Samoans who did so much towards spreading the faith could have done their work only if they had been utterly convinced of the truth and justice of their cause.

By the middle of the century the great days of the London Missionary Society in the Pacific may have been over, but there were now other missionary bodies to add their efforts to the spreading of Christianity. For example, the Presbyterians took over from the Rarotongan and Samoan teachers in the New Hebrides. Based on Scotland, and Australia and other Dominions, the Presbyterians had powerful backing from Australia, to such an extent that their missionaries were considered almost as unofficial Australian ambassadors. This was to come in very useful when the French Catholics began to compete with the Presbyterians in the New Hebrides. The Australians were able to protest with such conviction that the Catholics, who were finding it hard going anyway, left to concentrate their endeavours on New Caledonia, which was formally taken over by the French in 1853.

"Naliel addressing natives on board the *John Williams*." From *Gems from the Coral Islands, Volume I*, by the Rev. William Gill, Ward & Co. London, 1856. Naliel was one of four men of Erromanga persuaded in 1849 to voyage to Samoa where they took instruction in the word of God. In 1852 they returned to Erromanga in the *John Williams* though one of them died on the way. This sketch shows Naliel preaching to his fellow-islanders who had come on board to welcome their friends home to Erromanga.

The Roman Catholics were still active in smaller numbers throughout the Pacific. Other missionary societies tended to specialise, notably the Anglican Melanesian Mission, active in the Pacific since the early years of the century, but not to approach its full strength and power until the 1860s and later.

The Presbyterians in the New Hebrides and the Loyalty Islands were to start work with the arrival of John Geddie. The New Hebrides, among the wildest and most unhealthy of Pacific islands, its people dour and suspicious and given to cults and cannibalism, was not the ideal spot for missionary endeavour, as the Rarotongans and Samoans of the LMS had discovered to their cost. This did not deter John Geddie, the first Pacific missionary of the Presbyterian Church of Nova Scotia. Tough, humourless, single-minded and incredibly brave, he looked forward immensely to his new work and the battle that lay before him.

On the voyage out across the Atlantic and round the Horn, this craggy man wrote:

It is hard to realise the thought that I am really on my way to these beautiful realms where no Sabbath smiles on the beautiful people — where no congregations assemble to engage in the solemn services of religion, and where no preacher proclaims to them the good news of salvation, and warns them to flee from the wrath to come.

Accompanied by his wife, Geddie decided to establish his mission on the island of Aneityum, the most southerly of the islands of the New Hebrides. For a year he was accompanied by the Rev. T. Powell from the Samoan mission of the LMS. Powell, with that cooperation which marked the early years of Protestantism in the Pacific, was to act as adviser and helper for the first year. Unfortunately for the peace of mind of the two missionaries, as they approached the island for the first time in May they observed settlers already on Aneityum. Geddie described the initial shock:

By the aid of a spy glass we noticed some persons walking in front of it [an iron house], dressed in long priestly robes. In this we recognised at once the mark of the beast.

Actually the inoffensive perambulators were Marist priests, but to the stern Geddie they presented a dreadful sight. In fact they were to provide little opposition to the Presbyterian missionary. The eight priests and eight lay brothers were withdrawn to New Caledonia in 1850, and before they left they kindly invited Mrs Geddie to help herself to as much of their garden produce as she needed, an offer that was gratefully accepted.

Puritanical yet imaginative, Geddie made converts almost from the first. He even survived the blow of seeing the first Christian islander die within a short time of his conversion, an event that set the mission back considerably. Geddie's own child, Alexander, died of dysentery. The sandalwood traders, alarmed at having a man of Geddie's probity and strength of character in the neighbourhood, did their best to blacken his character among the natives and generally make his life a misery. Knowing that the missionary was a strict Sabbatarian, some traders shipping goods for the mission endeavoured to land them on a Sunday, knowing that it was almost certain to rain, but that the uncompromising

The Rev. John Geddie, DD. The frontispiece to *Missionary life among the cannibals*, by the Rev. George Patterson, Toronto, 1882.

Geddie would make no move to shift the goods from the beach until Monday, by which time they might be ruined.

In 1852 a Scottish Presbyterian, the Rev. John Inglis, and his wife also came to work at Aneityum, taking up residence on the other side of the island. By that year three buildings had been constructed on Geddie's station and he had imported a printing press and was labouring to learn the local language and translate the Bible into it. Such a gigantic undertaking could not be printed on the local press and the money had to be found to order from an overseas printer. For fifteen years the Christians on the island laboured to raise the money, collecting and selling arrowroot for the purpose and giving the money to the British and Foreign Bible Society.

The books of the mission reveal that after four years Geddie was responsible for a regular congregation of 350, 75 native assistants, 35 local schools and with almost 1,500 people, half the population, under instruction. Geddie and Inglis and their wives were the first unarmed white people to survive for any length of time in the New Hebrides. They owed a great deal to the chief Nohoat, who embraced Christianity and remained loyal to the faith against considerable opposition from other chiefs at first. Geddie was even able to send Aneityumese converts as teachers to other islands in the group. Some of these brave men were killed but some survived and taught.

After a time reinforcements came. From his native Nova Scotia the Rev. G. N. Gordon and his attractive wife sailed to the New Hebrides and established a mission on Erromanga in 1857. An enthusiastic and energetic man with many ideas, Gordon learned the language and local customs quickly. In one of his first sermons to the islanders he told them:

Religion may be compared to a coconut. The husk of ignorance must be removed and the hard shell of the love of sin must be broken by the hammer of the Word, ere the blessing could be obtained. . . .

A year after Gordon's arrival the Rev. J. G. Paton, a member of the Reformed Presbyterian Church of Scotland, and the Rev. J. W. Mathieson from Nova Scotia were stationed on Tanna. Paton was to become famous as a lecturer; he was a hardy, strong-minded missionary who did a great deal to combat the dreadful blackbirding slave trade in the Pacific.

The Gordons worked for four years until a sandalwood trading vessel brought an epidemic of measles to Erromanga. Many islanders died and the Gordons were blamed. The missionary wrote to his colleague Paton:

My Dear Brother,

I have news of the best and of the worst character to communicate. A young man died in December, in the Lord, as we believe. We are still preserved in health at our work by the God of all grace, whose power alone could have preserved us in all our troubles, which have come to us by the measles *per* the *Blue Bell*. Ah, this is a season which we will not soon forget. Some settlements are nearly depopulated and the principal Chiefs are nearly all dead! And oh, the indescribable fiendish hatred that exists against us! There is quite a famine here. The distress is awful, and the cry of mourning perpetual. A few on both sides of the Island who did not flee from the Worship of God are living, which is now greatly impressing some and exciting the enmity of others. I cannot now write of perils. We feel very anxious to hear from you. If you have to flee, Aneityum of course is the nearest and best place to which

you can go. Confidence in us is being restored. Mana, a native Teacher, remains with us for safety from the fury of his enemies. I cannot visit as usual. The persecution cannot be much worse on Tanna. I hope the worst is past. Mrs. G- unites in love to you, and to Mr. and Mrs. Johnston. In great haste,
I remain, dear Brother, Yours truly,
G. N. Gordon.

On 20 May 1861 he was lured from the printing office on some pretext by a chief named Lovu and his warriors, and was hacked down by tomahawks. Hearing the noise, his wife hurried from the mission house but was struck down from behind and killed before she could reach her husband's body.

Soon after this a sandalwood trader brought a party of Erromangans to Tanna where they tried to persuade the islanders to kill their missionaries, but the local people refused. The next day another band of natives, hearing of the death of the Gordons, besieged the Patons' mission house. Paton quotes the leader of the group as shouting:

The men of Erromanga killed Williams long ago. We killed the Rarotongan and Samoan teachers. We fought Turner and Nisbet [LMS missionaries], and drove them from our island. We killed the Aneityumese teachers on Aniwa, and one of Paton's teachers too. We killed several white men, and no man-of-war punished us. Let us talk over this, about killing Paton and the Aneityumese, till we see if any man-of-war comes to punish the Erromangans. If not, let us unite, let us kill these missionaries, let us drive the worship of Jehovah from our land!

Eventually the crowd dispersed leaving the Patons unmolested, but it had been an ugly incident. The arrival of a British man-of-war cooled matters; its commander called a meeting to determine the cause of the unrest and Nouka, an old man chosen as a spokesman, put into words what most of the islanders must have been feeling:

Captain Paddan and all the traders tell us that worship causes all our sickness and death. They will not trade with us, nor sell us tobacco, pipes, powder, balls, caps and muskets, till we kill our missi [missionary] like the Erromangans, but after that they will send a trader to live among us and give us plenty of these things. We love missi. But when the traders tell us that the worship makes us sick, and when they bribe us with tobacco and powder to kill him or drive him away, some believe them and our hearts do bad conduct to missi. Let missi remain here, and we will try to do good conduct to missi; but you must tell Queen 'Toria of her people's bad treatment of us, and that she must prevent her traders from killing us with their measles, and from telling us lies to make us do bad conduct to missi! If they come to us and talk as before, our hearts are very dark and may again lead us to bad conduct to missi.

These were bad days for the missionaries. War broke out between the local adherents of Christianity and the others, and the Patons and Mathiesons were forced to flee. Some of the islanders, in particular one man called Nowar, did a great deal to help them to escape on the *Blue Bell*. They joined Geddie on Aneityum, but both the Mathiesons fell ill and died within a short time of each other. Paton was prevailed upon by his colleagues to go on a fund-raising mission to Australia, and he sailed from the New Hebrides in 1862 with only the shirt and trousers he stood up in. His troubles were not yet over. The vessel in which he had taken his £10 passage to Sydney was a sandalwood trader whose captain had little time for missionaries. Between fist-fights with his mate and the steward, the captain occupied the only cabin with his island wife, and Paton had to sleep on the floor among the sandalwood, not taking off his clothes for the duration of the voyage of 1,400 miles, while his meals of execrable quality were served to him on deck.

Once in Australia, however, things took a turn for the better. Paton's dynamic personality, fund of nerve-racking stories and immense energy served him well on the lecture platform and at fund-raising meetings. He raised £5,000 on this tour and in succeeding years was to gather much more, certainly enough to pay for a mission ship, the *Dayspring*, built in Nova Scotia. The people of Australia, particularly the Presbyterians, rallied to the cause, and the Governor of Sydney himself presided at one meeting addressed by the missionary from the New Hebrides.

In 1865 Paton returned triumphantly to the New Hebrides in the *Dayspring*. Reinforcements had also arrived in the form of

Mission house at Aniwa. Frontispiece to *John G. Paton,* by
James Paton, London, 1889.

other European missionaries, including Morrison, McCullagh and
J. D. Gordon, the brother of the Gordon martyred on Erromanga;
in 1872 he was to share his brother's fate, killed by a native with
an axe.

Soon after Paton's return the islands were visited by a British
man-of-war, the *Curacao,* under Commodore Sir William
Wiseman. The vessel had been sent in answer to complaints from
both missionaries and traders about the unruly behaviour of the
natives. Wiseman decided to sail among the islands, investigating
the complaints, and asking some of the missionaries, Paton among
them, to accompany him as interpreters. The Commodore could
learn little from the islanders he succeeded in interviewing, but
decided that British subjects had indeed been troubled by the
natives. Accordingly he ordered the populations of two villages
to abandon their homes, and then shelled the villages. He also
sent working parties ashore to burn other villages. Few lives seem
to have been lost as a result of this punitive expedition, except

in the case of three islanders stripping the metal off an unexploded shell, who were killed when it suddenly blew up.

The visit of the *Curacao* was greeted with mixed feelings by the Europeans — some of the missionaries felt that the whole thing had been a ghastly mistake. Geddie, who had been away on leave, was especially bitter, and Paton received a great deal of blame, though he denied that he had had any hand in inviting Wiseman, and insisted that he had accompanied the *Curacao* only as interpreter.

Convinced that he was in the right, Paton did not allow the matter to upset him too much. Together with Copeland, Cosh and McNair and their wives, Mr and Mrs Paton sailed to open new mission stations on the islands. Paton and his wife settled on Aniwa, as their previous station on neighbouring Tanna was still considered too dangerous. Teachers from Aneityum had already done some preparatory work on the island and the Europeans were fairly well received. It appears that most of the islanders had now accepted, some with resignation, that the Presbyterians were going to be with them always. Life was not easy for the Patons on Aniwa, and on several occasions they were threatened by islanders; but the missionary and his wife refused to abandon the mission. By 1870 he had printed a hymn-book in the local language.

A church sixty-two feet by twenty-four was built by the islanders. It was levelled by a hurricane and Paton and the islanders rebuilt it. On one occasion he was attacked by an islander using a rifle as a club and was rescued by a band of women while his assailant fled into the bush. Somewhat shaken, he gathered the islanders together and warned them that if their behaviour did not improve he would go to another island where his life would be protected. The islanders conferred and then offered the missionary a bodyguard of 100 men. In 1873 Paton lost a child, his wife became very ill, and he almost died. He went to New Zealand on holiday, but left behind an island he could now claim as being converted.

Changes were taking place on other islands in the South Pacific. Following the establishment of the French protectorate over Tahiti in 1842, Queen Pomare was persuaded to return from self-imposed exile on Raiatea and to reign under the French. The Protestants also resigned themselves to working under a regime alien to them. In Britain George Pritchard, a Consul in exile, did his best to stir things up, but without much success. He received a small indemnity for the loss of his land in Tahiti, and was appointed Consul to Samoa at £300 a year. At about this time Henry Nott died. Once the most powerful man in Tahiti, he had in his lifetime seen the rise and fall of the London Missionary Society there and in the neighbouring islands.

There were scuffles between the Tahitians and the French, but the new overlords of the island were too well armed and disciplined for the islanders, and any trouble was soon put down. The French had promised religious toleration and the LMS missionaries laboured on, though aware that the great days were over. Roman Catholic missions were established, and agents of the Mormons also came to the Society Islands.

In 1848 a law was passed making churches and schools the property of the nation, and four years later legislation was brought down to ensure that ministers were elected by the leading men in each district. It was a far cry from the heyday of the LMS and the "missionary kingdom" of Tahiti. One by one the missionaries retired or died and were not replaced. In 1863 an agreement was reached by which French Protestants took over completely from the missionaries of the LMS. Queen Pomare ruled on under the French until her death in 1877, after a reign of fifty years. Her son, Pomare V, abdicated in favour of the French three years later. Catholics and Protestants lived in reasonable amity, but the "great days" of Christianity in the Society Islands were over.

The Wesleyans, working doggedly in the Friendly Islands, had good cause to be satisfied with their progress by 1835. Taufa'ahau, one of the most important chiefs had rallied to the Christian cause, and converts were being made. It was true that the Irishman Peter Dillon was urging the Catholics to penetrate the islands, but the Methodists were confident they could withstand outside pressure of that sort.

They were less impervious to pressure from within the islands. The heathen chiefs on Tongatabu were hostile and fiercely jealous of Taufa'ahau who had espoused the Christian cause. The

Christian islanders feared that civil war might result and built a fortress at Nuku'alofa. In 1837 it was besieged by rebel forces; the Christians stood fast, then launched a counterattack in which a number of the heathens were slaughtered. Afterwards Taufa'ahau came in for considerable criticism for his part in the massacres.

An uneasy peace reigned for a time but the Christians knew the pagan chiefs were sure to strike again. Both during the war of 1837 and the one that followed, the missionaries and their adherents were censured for their alleged part in the fighting, particularly by the Irishman Dillon. This led to the Rev. David Cargill publishing his *A Refutation of Chevalier Dillon's attacks on the Wesleyan Missionaries in the Friendly Islands,* part of which read:

> The Christians did not take up arms either to propagate their religion or establish heathenism. Their design was to suppress rebellion, maintain the authority to their legal monarch, to defend their rights and privileges, and to preserve their lives. Nor did they betake themselves to such an expedient, until every other means which their humanity and ingenuity could prompt, and their power compass, had proved unsuccessful. They did not betake themselves to it without repeated overtures of peace, pardon and reconciliation to the rebels; and even after they were prepared to act on the defensive, they lingered in unwillingness to engage in war, striving by manly and honourable means, to avert such a calamity; until their hopes were cut off, and their apprehensions realised by the commencement of hostilities on the part of the insurgents.

In October 1837, after the first war, the church members amounted to 1,056, an increase of eighty over the previous year. One hundred and twenty Tongans were on trial, seventy had left the church and eighty had died, including two local preachers killed in the war. There were fifteen schools with seventy-three teachers and 1,067 pupils. Throughout the period the missionaries laboured mightily at their daily tasks. The journal of one of them, the Rev. Stephen Rabone, shows us how a fairly typical day was spent:

> Wednesday, July 28, 1838. Yesterday morning, Mr. Tucker and I left Nuku'alofa for Hifiho; we arrived in the afternoon and made preparations for the baptisms. Early this morning,

Mr. Tucker preached; we then married several couples; after which we prayed. This ended, we catechised the candidates for baptism; and were well pleased with the manner in which they answered the questions in the presence of all the congregation; they then knelt down, and we proceeded to baptise them in the name of the Father, Son, and Holy Ghost. The first to whom this rite was administered was the old chief who embraced Christianity a few months back. . . . There were twenty or more at this place, and it was a most interesting occasion. After taking a little food, we came on to Teikiu, where there was another group in waiting. Being very many more than their small chapel would contain, the day being fine, I spoke to them outside the chapel enclosure. . . . I endeavoured to explain the nature and necessity of baptism in order to their receiving the Holy Ghost, so fully and graciously promised to them and their children, and all that are afar off. After sermon we married seven or eight couples, and then catechised the candidates; after which they all knelt down beneath the "spacious firmament" to receive the initiating rite, in the name of the ever-blessed Trinity. More than seventy have been baptised today, including children and young persons. We walked, in our return home, several miles through the tide, knee-deep, and the wind blowing very strong, so that it was only our upper garments that were at all dry. But praised be the Lord who has called up to our high and holy work.

In 1840 fighting broke out again between the Christians and heathens in the Friendly Islands; the incident sparking the conflict was provided when a heathen village accused neighbouring Christians of robbing their gardens, and killed a number of the converts in a pitched battle. Again Taufa'ahau rallied to the defence of the Christians, though he was by no means the king of Tonga, that position being occupied by King Joseph Tubou, who was only too pleased to receive the help of the fiery Taufa'ahau. On this occasion, remembering the severe criticism of his bloodthirsty tactics in the war of 1837, Taufa'ahau was more restrained, ordering his men to take prisoners wherever possible instead of slaughtering them indiscriminately.

On 24 April, while the hostilities were fairly lethargic, an unexpected visitor put in at Nuku'alofa with two ships. This was Commodore Wilkes of the United States Exploring Expedition. At first the missionaries welcomed the American and even acceded to his request that he be allowed to try to make peace between the two factions. When the Commodore interviewed a number of Tongans and announced that in his opinion the Christian side was as much to blame as the other, the attitude of the missionaries underwent a marked change. Coldly announcing that they had no need of the services of an ignorant outsider, they made it plain to Wilkes that his presence was no longer welcome. Washing his hands of the situation the American sailed his ships away, probably with some relief.

Less than a month later another naval visitor arrived, Captain Croker, in command of Her Majesty's sloop *Favourite*. The missionaries were not too keen on these visitors, but at least Croker was an Englishman and plainly would be on the side of order and Christianity. Tucker and Rabone thereupon asked him to help them against the heathens. The captain agreed promptly and marched a punitive force to the rebel headquarters at Bea, taking with him half his crew and three small guns.

Had it not been so tragic the situation would have been ludicrous. Croker, who had only recently picked up the bones of the martyred John Williams on Erromanga, led his small force on what was virtually a miniature Charge of the Light Brigade, anticipating that event by some decades. The rebels at Bea were well placed in a fort behind an earthen embankment twenty feet high, with the added defence of a ditch forty feet wide. The one entrance was barricaded with tree trunks. Even so, the islanders watched with some trepidation the advance of Croker's small force dragging the tiny fieldpieces and agreed at once when Croker came forward under a flag of truce and asked to be allowed to parley. Croker's terms, though delivered in a peremptory tone, were not unreasonable; merely that the fort be demolished and the islanders return to their villages. In turn, he promised that the Christian islanders would do the same. Where he made his mistake was to allow the islanders only thirty minutes to make up their minds — in a society where everything was settled by debate this was not nearly long enough.

Nevertheless the defenders had almost come to a decision to

abandon the fort when the thirty minutes were nearly up. Inside the fort were two British sailors, deserters, who were in charge of the primitive guns owned by the islanders. One of them, nicknamed Jimmy the Devil, was sent to the entrance to shout across to Croker, who was waiting with his force 100 yards away, requesting more time. Croker refused, afraid that this was a ruse to gain time for reinforcements to arrive. Standing with a watch in his hand he called off the remaining seconds and then began to run forward, crying out, "Now, men, follow me!"

The sight of the British sailors lumbering across the intervening ground was too much for the defenders: such an open target cried out to be demolished. Immediately they began firing their ancient muskets at the attackers. Almost at once Croker was shot and wounded. He stopped and leaned against a tree. Another shot struck him over the heart, killing him. Two of his men were fatally wounded and nineteen others injured; they wavered and broke, scuttling for safety, dragging their dead and wounded but leaving their artillery to be captured by the jubilant islanders.

The death of Croker virtually ended the war. The heathen islanders occupied Nuku'alofa while Taufa'ahau and his men retired circumspectly to the island of Vavau. The Governor of New South Wales conducted an inquiry into the death of Captain Croker, at which such embarrassing questions were asked as why, after dragging his artillery pieces so far and training them on the fort, the captain had never used them; and came to the conclusion that Croker had no business to get involved in a war in which Britain was not concerned, and that the unfortunate captain was to blame for the whole incident.

For some time the victorious side waited with apprehension for the arrival of a larger man-of-war to come and avenge the death of Croker, but none was sent. Even so the threat of such an occurrence was probably enough to persuade the victors to allow the missionaries to go about their work unmolested. This they proceeded to do, and soon largely forgot the embarrassment of having been on the losing side. In any case they had more important affairs to worry about, mainly the arrival of Roman Catholic priests who had been allowed to settle in the territory by Moeaki, a chief of the district of Bea, the area where the pagans had killed Croker.

On 30 June 1842 Bishop Pompallier, responding to a request from a number of chiefs, sent Father Joseph Chevron, who was accompanied by a lay brother. Another Marist priest joined them later in the year. The appearance of the Catholics drove the Methodists almost frantic, but there was little they could do. The chiefs who had invited the Frenchmen were jealous of the power of Taufa'ahau; now they had their own missionaries just as Taufa'ahau had his Wesleyans. The best the Methodists could do was to persuade the king to write to the Foreign Office in London, expressing his fears of a possible takeover by the French in Tonga, just as they appeared to be taking over Tahiti. The message was greeted with masterly indifference in England and in Tonga the missionaries of both faiths continued to eye each other with suspicion and dislike.

In 1845 the king died and Taufa'ahau was elected to his place. He ruled as King George Tubou I of the Tonga Islands, and lived to be ninety-six years old, perhaps the one Tongan who did most towards bringing his nation into the modern age. We retained a great deal of independence for Tonga at a time when other island territories were being taken over by the major European powers and the USA, which was now moving into the South Seas. Tubou was a highly intelligent man who had travelled around the Pacific and was well aware of the dangers looming up for a small island territory. He moved circumspectly at first. If his Wesleyan backers expected him to initiate a campaign against the Roman Catholics, they were disappointed. Tubou knew only too well that some chiefs would dearly like to take his crown, and that they would ally themselves with the Catholics in any religious struggle. He also knew that if the priests were annoyed or attacked, the French would send a naval force, just as they had to Tahiti, and that the independence of his country would be seriously threatened. As Tubou reiterated: ". . . it is not in my mind, nor in the mind of my people, that we should be subject to any other people or kingdom in the world".

In the meantime he was delighted to see the Methodist missionaries at work, and warmly welcomed the Rev. W. Lawry, one of the Wesleyan pioneers, who made a return visit to Tonga. In 1849 there was a school for local preachers at Nuku'alofa, conducted by Mr Amos, who gave an account of the life:

At the break of day the teachers all go to their gardens, and work until ten a.m.; each one stays at home in his turn to cook. At eight a.m., I conduct the children's school, with the assistance of two of the students, who all attend in turn. At the close of the children's school the teachers assemble for instruction until two o'clock. The afternoon they occupy in preparing the lessons for the morrow, bathing, bringing home food, attending to the means of grace &c.

The weekly routine of instruction embraces reading and analysis, writing and arithmetic, Bible-training lessons, sacred and general geography, natural history and philosophy, the English language, and traditions of Tonga. The latter branch is conducted in the form of conversations, which I write down in order to collect matter for a short history of the Friendly Islands, to be printed in Tonguese. Geometry and grammar I am preparing; but I find it exceedingly difficult to obtain suitable terms in Tonguese for definitions.

Another civil war broke out in 1852 between the king and Lavaka of the Bea area. To make matters worse Lavaka had been baptised a Catholic and the conflict began to take on the tones of a religious war. When the French priests made this accusation Tubou denied it roundly, pointing out that some Catholics were fighting on his side in what was purely a civil dispute. Tubou offered the priests at Bea safe escort to some other part of the island while the fighting was in progress, but they refused. The fighting — spasmodic, as was usually the case — went on for several months. A French vessel carrying the Roman Catholic Bishop of Samoa put in at Tonga and offered passage to the priests, but this offer was refused also. The ship sailed away but Tubou was convinced it would return with French reinforcements. As it happened, the next ship was a British man-of-war, HMS *Calliope* under Sir Everard Home, who offered to negotiate a peace settlement. Lavaka's warriors who were beginning to get the worst of the fighting, agreed. While the negotiations were taking place some of Tuhou's men broke into a fort belonging to the enemy and put it to the torch, burning a Catholic church in the process. But peace was made and the last civil war in Tonga was over.

Tubou, worried about the burning of the church, obtained from

Sir Everard a written acknowledgment that the king had done his best to protect the lives and property of the French priests in the area. The document was to come in useful when the inevitable French man-of-war turned up in November. The vessel was a little late by then. Tubou had offered generous terms to his defeated adversaries and a number of their leaders had become Methodists, being baptised by the missionaries. Belland, the French captain, conducted an investigation and expressed himself satisfied with the king's explanation. He went so far as to say to the interpreter:

Tell the king that I have known many chiefs in the South Seas, but I have never met his equal. The French acknowledge his authority as supreme ruler in Tonga. He must employ his authority in protecting all foreigners from insult, and must allow his subjects to choose what religion they please; but all must submit to the law of the land.

The king had cause to be pleased with his position: he had peace at home and a guarantee of immunity from the major predatory nation in the Pacific. Tubou was able to relax for a while. In 1852 he visited Sydney and was much impressed with what he saw. The aggressive monarch was not able to stay out of trouble for long, however: in 1855 he became involved in an odd religious war in Fiji.

Missionaries had been active in Fiji for some time before King George Tubou began to take an interest in the area. Some LMS Tahitian teachers had landed on the main island before 1830, but had not stayed long. John Williams expressed an evangelising interest in Fiji but agreed to give this up to the Methodists in return for a free hand for the LMS in Samoa. The first European missionaries to take up residence were the Wesleyans David Cargill and William Cross, both ordained ministers. They stayed first among the Lau Islands where there were many Tongans already amenable to Methodism. But the Methodists were to find their work extremely difficult: the Fijians were reluctant to give up their old gods and were lukewarm about the new religion. In 1844 two Roman Catholic priests, Fathers Bréhéret and Roulleaux, landed, but had as little success as the Methodists for many years.

"Fight between Fiji Islanders". A wood engraving in the
Alexander Turnbull Library, Wellington.

The turning point for the Methodists came in 1854 when a
leading chief, Cakobau, decided to become a Christian. He was
influenced in his decision by King George Tubou who, when
asked for help in a war by Cakobau, replied that he would do
so only if the chief became a Christian. The Methodist missionaries claimed that it was their efforts that had led to the conversion
of the Fijian leader, but there seems to have been more than a
tinge of political expediency about the move. Cakobau had
another stroke of good fortune when an American trader ran
his vessel past a blockade to land guns and supplies ordered by
the Fijian. These guns, and the Tongan warriors under the
gigantic and fearsome Tubou were enough to tilt the balance in
Cakobau's favour. The Wesleyans, though cautiously pleased
that a Christian, no matter how nominal, was now one of the most
important chiefs in Fiji, devoted most of their time to worrying
about the presence of the Catholics, fearing that the French might
attempt in Fiji what they had accomplished in Tahiti. Accordingly

the Methodists made the first of a number of requests for Britain to annexe Fiji. This first appeal was rejected.

The missionaries, both European and native, showed great courage. The Tongans and Fijians who acted as teachers usually went ahead of their white colleagues, and took the full impact of local opposition. Without these men the European missionaries would have had little chance of spreading the word of God. One of the most famous of the local teachers was the Tongan Joel Bulu, who worked for many years in Fiji and wrote a book about his experiences there. He gives an account of one inter-tribal battle and its aftermath, the like of which he was forced to witness many times:

Well do I remember the day that Bau and Viwa had smitten Teilau, the little island opposite Viwa which stands empty at this day — how a large war-canoe came in laden with the dead, who were taken ashore and piled up in a great heap on the low flat opposite to our houses; and when the Bau mesesnger had finished his report the king said "Do what you like with them", whereupon there rose a sudden yell. A great rush was made down to the waterside and the bodies were dragged hither and thither as the people struggled with one another over them, many clutching the same body, cutting them up limb from limb, tearing them asunder, and snatching the pieces out of one another's hands. And the yells rose louder and louder as the people grew ever fiercer in their eagerness; women and children also mingled with them in the struggle, their shrill voices rising high amid the uproar.

When Cakobau, aided by his Tongan allies, succeeded in defeating his adversaries, he was true to his promise and became a Christian, taking the name of Ebenezer. Cakabou was disliked and feared by many of the European settlers on Fiji and received little help from them — indeed for a long time his only friends seemed to be the Methodist missionaries. By this time many white men were beginning to make their homes on Fiji, establishing trading posts and running sugar plantations. Britain sent a Consul to the island, W. T. Pritchard, son of the former Tahitian mission-ary. The United States, France, and Germany began to take an interest in the area and an increasing number of men-of-war of different nations started to visit Fiji. Some of the settlers were

"A missionary meeting at Fiji." A wood engraving in the Alexander Turnbull Library,

law-abiding enough, but the islands became notorious in the second half of the nineteenth century as a haunt of desperadoes. By 1874, when Fiji was ceded to Britain, there were about 2,500 whites there; and by that time the missions had lost a great deal of their power.

The Catholics in Fiji had not had an easy time in establishing their mission, but in other parts of the South Pacific they were beginning to make considerable headway. The Marists, controlled from France by their dedicated and efficient Superior General, Jean Claude Colin, and administered in the field by such men as Bishop Bataillon, were making up for their comparatively late arrival in the Pacific with their determination and courage. After a dreadful start they were particularly successful on Wallis and Futuna and were able to use these tiny islands as springboards for other ventures in Melanesia and Polynesia.

Bishop Pompallier, harassed, overworked and lacking administrative skills, had landed Father Chanel and Brother Nizier on the minute volcanic Futuna on the first Marist expedition across the Pacific. It had been an action taken almost on the spur of the moment when the vessel carrying the priests had put in to land a European beachcomber.

"I am obliged to follow God's designs step by step," Pompallier had written desperately, "and they disclose themselves only from day to day in the opportunities it pleases Him to offer me."

In all good faith Pompallier told the islanders that he would return in six months, but when he failed to do so the men of Futuna concluded that Pierre Chanel had been abandoned by the white men and was therefore someone of little consequence. They stole the priest's food and, on 28 April 1841, murdered him.

On Wallis, the equally small Polynesian island, Bataillon had more success, and, thanks to his dogged efforts, by 1845 both Wallis and Futuna had been Christianised. Bataillon used the mission on Wallis to supply priests and native missionaries for other Pacific islands, sending them to Tonga, Fiji and Samoa. On the latter island he had some success initially through two Wallis women who had married Samoans. The Samoan men adopted the Catholic religion of their wives and took their faith home with them.

"Natives of Footoona." From *Missions in Western Polynesia,*
by A. W. Murray, John Snow, London/G. R. Addison, Sydney,
1863.

New Caledonia, too, became Catholic, thanks to the work of
Bishop Douarre and others. At one point, however, the Catholics
had to abandon the island when their mission was attacked and
a brother killed. Douarre was away in Europe at the time but
the others were saved by the opportune arrival of a French
man-of-war. Douarre judged it expedient to withdraw his mission
temporarily to the neighbouring Isle of Pines. Fifty New
Caledonian converts accompanied the mission and this gave
Douarre the idea of sending some of them to Futuna for basic
theological training. On completion of their instruction these
selected islanders were sent back to their homes on New Caledonia
in a second attempt, this time successful, to start a Catholic
mission. After a great deal of consideration following the murder
of Bishop Epalle, the Solomons were abandoned as too difficult
for the time being.

In France Colin was struggling to find money to enable his
missionaries to do their work in the Pacific islands. In thirteen
years he sent more than a hundred missionaries from Europe to
the Pacific, and his priests were to work in New Caledonia,

Pierre Chanel, martyred on Futuna.
Frontispiece to *Ecrits du Père Pierre
Chanel,* Paris, 1860.

Wallis, Futuna, Tonga, Fiji and Samoa. By 1849, however, the
Marist Superior General had decided he could no longer afford
to send more missionaries to the Pacific. It was a decision that
cost Colin a great deal:

I have loved these missions. Nobody has wanted their success,
their prosperity, more than I. It is not the cannibalism of the
savages that has arrested the missionary impulse and numbers.
The misfortune has another cause. God has allowed it, reserving
undoubtedly more abundant blessings for them in the future.

The Marists who remained continued their work among the
islands, and were joined by colleagues from other orders. Later
the Marists began to send missionaries to the area again; but by the
end of the century they had returned to the Solomons, among
other places.

One remote Pacific island that embraced Christianity in an
unusual almost bizarre way was Pitcairn, the island on which
some of the survivors of the *Bounty* mutineers, together with a
number of Tahitian men and women, had settled in an attempt
to hide from the British naval vessels. Before long the Tahitian
men and the British mutineers had fallen out over the women
and had begun to kill one another. Eventually only two sailors

and a number of Tahitian women were left alive, but these were enough to propagate and found an English-speaking community.

One of the survivors "found religion", and the Pitcairners built their own church. The succeeding generations became extremely devout people. Then, in the 1820s, the island received a visit from one of those unusual characters to be found in some numbers in the Pacific in the nineteenth century. This was George Hunn Nobbs, an Irishman, ex-seaman in the British Navy, one-time "freedom-fighter" against the Spanish in South America, occasional buccaneer and three times a convict in various prisons. Nobbs turned up at Pitcairn in the company of one Noah Bunker, who several times tried to commit suicide and then died. Neither man gave any reason for their unexpected arrival in a twenty-ton vessel, but before his death Bunker in a loose moment disclosed: "As you may imagine, the reasons were very powerful ones, but I cannot tell you what they were."

After Bunker's death Nobbs showed no inclination to leave. Indeed he begged so hard to be allowed to stay, and his general manner had been so pious and subdued, that the islanders allowed him to remain as a teacher for their children. After a time he began to conduct prayer meetings at his house. Moerenhout, the ubiquitous Belgian pearl-trader, visited Pitcairn at this time, and though suspicious of Nobbs's obscure background, admitted that he was a quiet man who conducted himself in a respectable manner.

Moerenhout did point out that Nobbs, without apparently meaning to do so, seemed to sow the seeds of dissension and make people unhappy with their lot. The Belgian's assessment seemed accurate when, in 1831, Nobbs persuaded a number of the young Pitcairners to sail with him to Tahiti to start a new life there. The emigration proved short-lived. When the puritanical Pitcairners arrived at Tahiti not only did they discover that a civil war was about to break out, but a number of friendly, perhaps over-friendly, young women boarded the Pitcairners' vessel and so shocked the young men that their whole sojourn got off to a bad start. Nobbs and the Pitcairners stayed only five months on Tahiti, during which time twelve of their number died. Then the chastened survivors accepted a generous donation of

650 Spanish dollars from the LMS missionaries and chartered a vessel to take them back to Pitcairn.

No sooner had they arrived than Nobbs was in trouble again. By this time the Irishman was acting as semi-official if unqualified minister to the Pitcairners. In 1832 another eccentric European landed at Pitcairn, a man called Hill, who claimed to be closely related to various members of the British aristocracy and to have been sent to Pitcairn on an important but highly secret mission. At first Nobbs welcomed the Englishman and even put him up in his own house before he discovered he was nurturing a viper in his bosom.

Joshua Hill turned out to be a fanatic. In no time at all he declared himself virtual dictator of Pitcairn. Accusing Nobbs of drunkenness, he dismissed him from his pastor's post and even had him removed from his own house. The placid and bewildered islanders did not know what to do. Hill had set himself up as their spiritual as well as temporal leader and was busy issuing edicts of various kinds. Some books were banned, a prison built, land ordinances introduced and opponents of the new regime flogged. To cap it all, Hill gave himself the title "President of the Commonwealth".

It must have been a bewildering experience for Nobbs and the Pitcairners. Only a few short years before all had been peaceful under the patriarch John Adams, sole survivor of the *Bounty* mutineers. Now they were living in a veritable nightmare. Fortunately for Nobbs, a vessel bound for Tahiti with some LMS missionaries put in at Pitcairn and he was able to escape on that, together with other residents who had incurred the wrath of Hill.

The Tahitian missionaries took pity on Nobbs; further, they were impressed by his personality and apparent convictions. They sent him to the Gambier Islands, some three hundred miles from Pitcairn, to help one of their missionaries there. Here Nobbs came into contact with some of the first Roman Catholic missionaries in the Pacific, the Jesuits Caret, Laval, and Columban. Nobbs seems to have been kind to the new arrivals, offering them his own hut until they had built their own.

Back on Pitcairn, Hill finally went too far. After a twelve-year-old girl had been accused of stealing yams the dictator declared that she should be executed. This was too much even for the

The Rev. G. H. Nobbs. From the *Mutineers of the Bounty*, by Lady Belcher, New York, 1871.

pacific Pitcairners. They turned against Hill, who promptly attacked one with a sword, but was overpowered. He was shipped out of the island in 1838 and the relieved islanders petitioned Nobbs to return, offering to pay his fare. The Irishman needed no second bidding and came back eagerly, settling down once more as the island's pastor. He worked extremely hard with his flock. In 1850 Walter Brodie visited the island and left an account of what he saw, declaring that "there never was, and perhaps never will be, another community who can boast of so high a tone of morality, or more firmly rooted religious feelings than our worthy and true friends, the Pitcairn Islanders".

Brodie went on to say that Nobbs was treated with great respect by the Pitcairners and that he acted as their pastor in all things except that as he was not in holy orders he did not administer the Eucharist. Brodie did point out, however:

Before quitting the church, I must mention that, although Mr. Nobbs has been of the greatest service to these islanders, he is now getting old and infirm, and ought to be allowed to retire, and his place occupied by a minister, if possible in holy orders, and one who knows a little of medicine; and this ought to be carried into effect immediately, either by Her Majesty's Government, or some laudable religious society.

If Nobbs ever saw these remarks they must have caused him some amusement, for the Irishman had hardly started his career. A year or so after Brodie had urged him to retire, Nobbs was on his way to Britain in HMS *Portland,* commanded by Admiral Fairfax Moresby, who had been greatly taken by the Irishman's engaging air and was to act as his patron. In Britain Nobbs took a curtailed course for the ministry and in 1852 was "licensed to perform the Office of Chaplain to the Inhabitants of Pitcairn's Island". He was made much of and even granted an audience by Queen Victoria.

He returned to Pitcairn in May 1853, an ordained minister at last. For many men it would have been the prelude to a graceful retirement. Not so for Nobbs. In 1856 he was to lead a large part of his flock on yet another exodus, this time to Norfolk Island. Here the Irishman was to come into contact with Bishop Selwyn of the Anglican Melanesian Mission, perhaps the most important and successful missionary organisation of the second half of the nineteenth century in the Pacific.

Samuel Marsden (1765-1838).

7

MISSION TO MELANESIA

The Church of England, in the form of the Church Missionary Society, came to New Zealand in 1814 when Samuel Marsden brought some lay brothers from Sydney, preached a Christmas sermon and then left the brothers to get on with the work of founding a Church in the young country. By 1823 Henry Williams, a former officer in the British Navy, was in charge of the expanding mission in a land that was lawless in the extreme. For a long time but with only minimal success the Church Missionary Society struggled to minister both to the white adventurers and the bewildered Maoris. In 1841 fresh urgency and sense of purpose were injected into the mission when George Augustus Selwyn, then only a year or two over thirty, was appointed Bishop of New Zealand and travelled from England to his new territory.

Selwyn, fit, vigorous, and autocratic, had been educated at Eton and St John's, Cambridge, where he was Second Classic in the classical tripos and rowed number seven in the first university boat race. For ten years after he had taken his degree he combined being a private tutor at Eton with a number of honorary curacies and some parish work. His father had been one of the Prince Consort's advisers on law and constitution and Selwyn was not a poor man — nor without influential friends. His was a privileged existence and one that brought him to the notice of a number of Church leaders culminating in the offer, while still a young man, of the important and onerous post of Bishop of New Zealand. Convinced that he had experienced a call, Selwyn accepted, preached a farewell sermon at Exeter Cathedral on the theme "How shall we sing the Lord's song in a strange land", and left with his wife for his new life.

He discovered that in addition to New Zealand his diocese also included the Melanesian islands. This, one story goes, was because of a clerical error, a slip of the pen which gave into Selwyn's care the area from 50 degrees south to 34 degrees north, instead of to 34 degrees south, as had been the intention. Selwyn willingly accepted the islands of Melanesia as part of his see, though for the first five or six years in New Zealand he was unable to pay much attention to the Pacific. His early years in New Zealand were busy, fruitful and marked by controversy. Physically the Bishop was in his element, revelling in the long hours and extensive walking involved in touring his diocese. The work was made even more difficult by the shortage of skilled helpers. There was also a distressing incident in which Henry Williams, virtually the founder of the Church in New Zealand, was accused, falsely it is now considered, of owning too much land, and ordered to give it up. Williams was also dismissed from the Church Missionary Society, though he was later reinstated. Throughout this matter Selwyn appears to have been overworked and rather out of touch; it was an episode reflecting little credit on anyone concerned.

Most of Selwyn's work in New Zealand, however, was of the highest standard. He did invaluable work among the Maoris, founded St John's College for both white and coloured students, and toured the country extensively. By 1847 he was ready to turn to the Melanesian islands for which he was responsible. In that year he was able to visit them in the capacity of chaplain to HMS *Dido*, which was sent to Rotuma and Granville to investigate reports of fighting between the natives and the crews of visiting ships. At this time the Melanesian islands, particularly the Solomons, were practically unknown. Selwyn was much impressed by the opportunities for evangelism in Melanesia, and later wrote:

> While I have been sleeping in my bed in New Zealand, these Islands — the Isle of Pines, New Caledonia, New Hebrides, New Ireland, New Britain, New Guinea, the Loyalty Islands, the Kingsmills, &c. — have been riddled through and through by the whale-fishers and traders of the South Seas. That odious black slug, the beche-de-mer, has been dragged out of its hole in every coral reef, to make black broth for Chinese Mandarins by the unconquerable daring of English traders, while I, like a worse black slug as I am, have left the world all its field of worship to itself. The same daring men have robbed every one of the islands of its sandal-wood, to furnish incense for the idolatrous worship of the Chinese temples, before I have taught a single islander to offer up his sacrifice of prayer to the true and only God. Even a mere Sydney speculator could induce nearly a hundred men from some of the wildest islands in the Pacific to sail in his ship to Sydney to keep his flocks and herds, before I, to whom the Chief Shepherd has given commandment to seek out His sheep that are scattered over a thousand isles, have sought out or found so much as one of those which have strayed and are lost.

Selwyn may have been late in turning his attention to Melanesia, but he made up for lost time when he turned his mind to the establishment of the Melanesian Mission. From 1849 to 1859, except for one three-year period when he was in Britain, Selwyn managed to pay at least one visit a year to the Melanesian islands. He brought young men and boys from the islands to attend school for part of the year in New Zealand, returning them to their homes to spread the word of God. Like the missionaries of the LMS he tried to establish efficient trading practices wherever he went. As he said once on Guadalcanal:

> I give most of my goods to those who give me in turn what I want. Now what I want is to take some of your young people . . . I want intelligent young lads, who can learn new habits and listen to a new teaching.

During his period in England in 1853, Selwyn set out to look for an assistant, someone who could eventually take over the running of the Melanesian Mission, "with the hope of a Missionary Bishop to take the work off my hands at some future time". His choice fell on a young curate, John Coleridge Patteson, the man who became the first Bishop of Melanesia.

Patteson was as interesting a character as Selwyn, and not unlike his mentor in background. Born in 1827, the son of a judge, he spent his early years amid the trappings of wealth. When he was eleven he was sent to Eton. He appears to have been a normal, pleasant boy, not a great scholar but good at games and with plenty of self-confidence. He became captain of cricket and a member of the debating society. As a young man he was pleasant but indolent.

One of the turning points in his life came at the age of fourteen, when he heard a sermon preached by Samuel Wilberforce, then Archdeacon of Surrey and a future bishop. The sermon that day dealt with the work of God overseas, and it affected the young Patteson greatly. Wilberforce's text was taken from John 12: 20 and 21: "Neither pray I for these alone, but for them also which shall believe on me through their word; that they all may be one; as Thou, Father, art in me, and I in Thee, that they also may be one in us: that the world may believe that Thou hast sent me."

On the same day, John Coleridge Patteson heard another sermon, this time at Windsor, delivered by Bishop Selwyn, then on his way to New Zealand for the first time. Selwyn was a friend of an uncle of Patteson's and later the engrossed boy was to be allowed to see the letters written from New Zealand by the Bishop. Patteson wrote:

I heard Archdeacon Wilberforce in the morning and the bishop in the evening, though I was forced to stand all the time. It was beautiful when he talked of his going to found a Church, and then to die neglected and forgotten. All the people burst out crying, he was so very much beloved by his parishioners. He spoke of his perils, and putting his trust in God; and then when he had finished, I think I never heard anything like the sensation, a kind of feeling that if it had not been on so sacred a spot all would have exclaimed "God bless him!"

The Rt Rev. George Angustus Selwyn. From *History of the Melanesian Mission,* by E. S. Armstrong, Ibister & Co., Ltd, London, 1900.

Selwyn appears to have been a little premature in his account of perils and dangers as he had not even left Britain at this time, but his sermon had an impressive effect on the youthful Patteson. It was to be some years, however, before he was to spend the rest of his life in the Pacific. In 1845 he left Eton and spent three years at Balliol College, Oxford, where he took his degree — the men of the Melanesian Mission, it may be seen, had vastly different backgrounds than their forerunners of the London Missionary Society. After Oxford Patteson toured Switzerland and Italy, during which time he showed that he had a gift for languages by learning German, Hebrew, and Arabic. For a year he returned to Oxford and was then ordained a priest in the Church of England.

Patteson spent twelve months in charge of a parish and then met Bishop Selwyn again. By this time Selwyn, who was in England raising funds and looking for an assistant, was renowned for his work in New Zealand and particularly in Melanesia. In 1852 he had cruised among the Solomon and Santa Cruz islands, performing nineteen baptisms: in four years he had visited more than fifty islands in Melanesia. Patteson volunteered to go to New Zealand and was accepted by the older man. On 6 July 1855 Bishop Selwyn and his new assistant, John Coleridge

Patteson, landed in New Zealand. Patteson began his work almost
at once, learning the Maori language in order to preach in that
tongue.

It was about this time that they came into contact with George
Nobbs, late of Pitcairn. Nobbs had brought a considerable number
of Pitcairners to the former convict settlement on Norfolk Island,
north-west of New Zealand, and most of them had settled in quite
happily. Selwyn had hoped to use this island as the base for a
school of his own, but it was to be some years before he was
able to do so. In the meantime he struck up an amicable relationship with the Irish minister.

In 1856 Bishop Selwyn took Patteson on his first tour of the
Melanesian islands. The object of the voyage was the usual one
— to collect island boys and take them to New Zealand for
training. The first island to be visited was Rennell, a Polynesian
outlier of the Solomon Islands. They were greeted with enthusiasm
by the friendly Polynesians who swarmed all over the mission
ship; many of the Rennellese spent the night on board, and it is
on record that they sang to Selwyn and Patteson the *kaka* — the
song of love.

This first voyage of Patteson's was a great success. Occasionally
he came across a grim reminder of local customs; on San
Cristobal, for example, he and Selwyn were taken to a council
house in which there were twenty-eight skulls as proof of the
headhunting prowess of the villagers. But most of the stops were
pleasanter affairs. They were well received on Guadalcanal and
Malaita, and then sailed down to the Santa Cruz islands and on
to the Banks before returning to New Zealand. There Patteson
began to teach at the Diocese of Melanesia's school in Auckland,
where Melanesian students ,among others, received instruction.
The priest grew very fond of his island charges and wrote of
them:

> They are such dear fellows, and I trust they already begin to
> know something of religion. Certain it is that they answer readily
> questions, and say with their mouths what amounts almost to
> a statement of the most important Christian truths. Of course
> I cannot tell what effect this may have on their hearts. They
> join in prayer morning and night, they behave admirably and
> really there is nothing in their conduct to find fault with. If

it please God that any of them were at some future time to stay again with us, I have great hopes that they may learn enough to become teachers in their own country.

Patteson was a popular and effective teacher, in many ways ahead of his time. He wanted no discrimination between Melanesians and Europeans, yet at the same time did not want to Anglicise the islanders. With Bishop Selwyn he believed that the customs of the Melanesians should, wherever possible, be retained within the tradition of the Church. Patteson decided that Motu should be the medium of instruction and learned the language himself. When he went to the Solomons to return the students he had collected with Selwyn, his progress was triumphant.

Canoes came out to greet him at almost every stop. He slept ashore on Guadalcanal, probably the first white man to do so since the days of Mendana's Spaniards 300 years before. His ship was visited by 450 natives, five of them great chiefs. In 1857 Patteson called at sixty-six islands, effected eighty-one landings and brought away thirty-three pupils, chiefly from San Cristobal and Guadalcanal. This was the beginning of many such voyages. His skill as a navigator developed and his physical strength was put to good use on many occasions when he was forced to swim ashore from the mission ship because a boat could not penetrate a reef or there were no canoes to carry him. Eventually he made this his practice, ordering the ship to wait some distance out, and then swimming ashore, carrying an armful of presents.

At the school in New Zealand Patteson worked from 5.30 in the morning until past 10 at night. He deplored rapid conversions and would accept no boy into the Christian faith until convinced that he was sincere. Some came to the school from the islands more than once: a famous student was William Didimang from San Cristobal in the Eastern Solomons. Didimang was away from his village when the *Southern Cross* put in to pick up any students, but later a trading ship arrived and the captain promised to take Didimang and his companion, the son of the chief Iri, to New Zealand. Instead the two bewildered Solomon Islanders were taken to China where they were abandoned. His companion died, and he buried him, then worked his passage to New Zealand on another vessel and turned up at the school ready for his lessons.

Later Patteson travelled to San Cristobal to break the news of

John Coleridge Patteson. Engraving after a sketch by George Richmond, RA. Frontispiece to *Life of John Coleridge Patteson*, by C. M. Yonge, London, 1874.

the death of Iri's son to the chief. The women of the village sang a lament and, according to custom, the men broke a plank from the youth's canoe, because now he would have no more use for it. Iri sat apart and no-one was able to console him. Patteson spoke to the villagers on the beach, and his words have survived:

The son of your chief is dead. This is true. He will never come back to Bauro. He wanted to come to New Zealand to school there, but he died before he could get there. Why did he want to go to the school? Why do I come to the islands every year to fetch your young men to the school? I do not come here to exchange fishhooks and hatchets for yams and taro. I do not come here just to give your young men a chance to see other lands. I fetch them so that I may try to teach them the knowledge of the Great Father in Heaven and of His son Jesus Christ, so that they may be happier hereafter. You and your young men are not like birds and beasts which perish, but some day all of you will rise and live for ever if you believe in God. And to live with the great God in happiness you must stop fighting and hatred and stealing so that you may live in peace, just as the son of Iri the chief is now in peace.

Patteson later saw to it that a church was built in the village, and afterwards Iri himself became a Christian. Still the students continued to come from the islands for part of each year. The location of the school was transferred to Norfolk Island. For five years Patteson worked there, interspersed with tours of the islands. Then it was decided that the time had come for him to take over the responsibility of the Church in the islands from Selwyn. On St Matthias' Day, Sunday, 24 February 1861, John Coleridge Patteson, then thirty-four years old, was consecrated first Bishop of Melanesia.

For the ten remaining years of his life Bishop Patteson worked in the islands. He established his headquarters at Mota in the Banks group, of which he was very fond, often speaking of "the dry soil, the spring of water, the wondrous fertility of the soil, the large and remarkably intelligent, well-looking population, the great banyan tree, twenty-seven paces round. . . ." Patteson was fond of this tree, which is found in some profusion in the Pacific, and used it as a symbol of his constant touring, speaking of "my cathedral, the banyan tree". Always Patteson toured, looking for fresh islands to visit, until he was able to say:

It pleased God to prosper us beyond all our utmost hopes. I was not only able to land on many places where no white man had set foot before, but to go inland, as at Santa Cruz, to sit for hours among a throng of people as at Raga. From eight islands have we for the first time received boys for our school, and fifty-one Melanesian men, women and boys are now with us, gathered from twenty-four islands. At Santa Cruz, where we have never landed before, I was permitted to go ashore at seven places, during which I saw about twelve hundred men. Though in all these islands the inhabitants are wild, naked, armed with spears and clubs or bows and arrows, and scenes of violence and bloodshed are frequent, yet through-out this voyage, during which I landed between seventy and eighty times, not one hand was lifted up against me, not one sign of ill-will exhibited.

It was a singularly happy situation, but one that was doomed. By the middle of the nineteenth century the sandalwood traders and the whalers had been replaced in the Pacific by a far crueller and more avaricious set of men — the blackbirders. From about 1847 the cotton and sugar plantations of Fiji and Queensland had been demanding labour, men capable of working for long hours in the blazing sun. High prices were to be paid for such labourers. Scoundrels of the calibre of Bully Hayes and Ross Lewin set out to provide this work force, landing at the islands of Melanesia in search of slaves. The scum of the earth came to the Pacific in search of easy money in the blackbirding trade; shipowners and seamen came from Australia, Britain, the USA, France, and Germany.

The methods of attracting potential labourers to leave their island villages varied. Sometimes presents were given to the men, or more often to the village headmen, to persuade the ignorant islanders to agree to a contract which would condemn them to anything from one to six years in Fiji or Australia, usually for a wage of less than £1 a month. When islanders could not be bribed or tricked, they were often kidnapped. Gangs of white seamen would go ashore at a village and carry off men and youths at gunpoint. One British naval officer gave an account of this despicable trade in 1871:

The traders take the natives to Queensland and Fiji and get so much a head for what is called "passage money" which varies from £4.10s. to £6.10s. a head. No less than thirteen English vessels have been engaged in taking away natives from Lifou and Maré since May 1865 — nearly all from Sydney. These vessels clear out ostensibly for the beche-de-mer and coconut-oil trade, but in many cases their real cruise is after natives, whom they seduce by false promises and often capture by violence and then run them across to Brisbane in Queensland, or to the Fiji Islands.

The main arm of the law in the Pacific was the British Navy, but its officers were severely limited in their powers. They could administer punishment to native offenders by an "Act of War", which allowed them to burn villages and hang islanders judged to be guilty of endangering the lives of Europeans. But white offenders could only be arrested — if caught — and taken to New South Wales to stand trial. Most naval officers felt that their hands were tied when it came to apprehending blackbirders.

In 1869 HMS *Rosaria* under the command of Captain George Palmer was sent to the Pacific to inquire into the kidnapping of natives. He soon had a doleful tale to relate as he toured the islands and talked to the missionaries. At New Caledonia the French governor declared that the Protestant missionaries were conniving at the traffic in slaves until Palmer was able to prove that the Presbyterian Church of Scotland had demanded an official investigation.

From New Caledonia Palmer sailed to Aneityum where he met the almost legendary Geddie who had already been in the New Hebrides for twenty-one years. Geddie was strong in his denunciation of the blackbirders. He said that the natives refused to have anything to do with the missionaries or any other white men because so many of their villagers had been kidnapped. At Espiritu Santo, the chief had even refused a present, an unheard-of occurrence, so terrified was he of white men. Again and again islanders had informed Geddie that so many of their people had been stolen that they were afraid to approach the beach.

Palmer received the same information from the Rev. Mr Neilson on Tanna, who added that the blackbirders were giving chiefs muskets and ammunition in return for persuading their young men to go to Queensland and Fiji. These firearms, the minister feared, would be used with dreadful effect in intertribal warfare. Neilson was able to produce a man called Yaufangan who confessed that he had persuaded twenty-four men to embark on the notorious blackbirding vessel *Young Australian*.

Grimly Palmer sailed on to Erromanga where the missionary in residence, McNair, had two chiefs, Numpunara and Loetevon, waiting with their evidence. They claimed that a blackbirding vessel had called at the island the previous September and offered liberal supplies of tobacco in exchange for sandalwood. When some canoes had paddled out to the vessel ten natives were seized and hustled below decks as the ship sailed away. Another islander claims that five more natives had been abducted by the same vessel at Dillon's Bay, and a woman stated that nine other islanders had been lured on board by the promise of a gift of pigs, and had then been hustled below and the hatches secured.

Cosh, the missionary on Vaté, though admitting that there had been no blackbirding raids on his island, complained about the

"Aneiteumese Heathen Village." From *Missions in Western Polynesia*, by A. W. Murray, John Snow, London/G. R. Addison, Sydney, 1863.

plight of those labourers who had left voluntarily on one-year contracts for Queensland or Fiji. He said that some islanders had been detained against their wishes for as long as three years, and that at least one man had been given up for lost and had eventually returned to find his wife living with another man.

Everywhere on his fact-finding tour Palmer encountered similar stories and situations. In Fiji the captain commented: "Some of the planters settled in these islands are gentlemen, with whom I had the pleasure of becoming acquainted; others, and at present, I am sorry to say, the majority, are the biggest scoundrels unhung." He gained more confirmation of the tactics of the slave traders when he questioned island labourers in the sugarfields.

Later he arrested a notorious blackbirder, but the man was acquitted before a court in New South Wales and Palmer himself forced to pay the costs of the case, some £179, though the sum was later refunded to him by the British Government.

Occasionally the kidnapped natives attempted to escape from the blackbirding vessels. One such endeavour was described in the *Fiji Times,* dated 9 October 1869. The sympathies of the newspaper were heavily on the side of the blackbirders.

The *Mary Anne Christina* arrived in Levuka harbour on Thursday from the Line Islands, and Captain Field brings the sad news of the massacre by natives of the captain and first mate of the French barque *Moorea,* and Mr. Latin, who was on board; also the wholesale loss of life of the savage murderers by drowning in trying to make the land by swimming ashore. The following are the particulars as given us by Captain Field.

On the arrival of the *Mary Anne Christina* at the island of Porou, on the 27th August, two white men, named Antoni and Slater, informed Captain Field that a week or two previous to his arrival a sad calamity had occurred in the murder of three white men and the drowning of 250 natives. It seems that these two men witnessed from the beach the barque a few miles from the shore, at the mercy of the winds and waves, and what seemed to them a confusion on board the vessel. The next day the barque was out of sight, but later in the day some thirty natives reached the shore, greatly exhausted, having been in the water since the day previous. From these natives it was gathered that they had risen in a body, surprised the captain and Mr. Latin, knocked them down, cut their heads nearly off, and thrown them into the sea. The first mate and a native named Sandy pulled out their revolvers, and shot the natives down in all directions, the mate accidentally shooting his subordinate Sandy, who immediately made below; the mate met the same fate as the captain shortly afterwards. The second mate, the natives say, ran below and hid himself. The murderers, finding the vessel leaving the land fast, all jumped into the sea and made for the shore, only thirty reaching the land out of some 280. . . .

Small wonder that the islanders became increasingly hostile to all white men, the missionaries included. Bishop Patteson himself was attacked on Santa Cruz in 1864, though previously he had been able to land there unmolested. On this occasion the Bishop had gone ashore in the ship's boat with two other missionaries and three Norfolk Islanders. After walking about for some time, the visitors returned to their boat and began to head back for the mission vessel. Crowds of islanders appeared on the reef and began firing arrows at the party in the boat. Three of them were struck and two of them, Norfolk Islanders died later. Patteson was unhurt, but it had been a close call.

While the situation in the islands was becoming crucial, the school on Norfolk Island flourished. Patteson sank over £1,000 of his own money into the school and its grounds. He took no salary. The mission was supported partly by the money left to Patteson by his father, partly from his stipend as a Fellow of Merton College, and partly by funds raised by the Eton Melanesian Society and an association formed in Australia. Patteson kept as his aim the localisation of the Church in Melanesia. He wanted the islanders eventually to run their own churches.

Almost inevitably his health suffered as a result of constant overwork. The other bishops in New Zealand petitioned him to rest, but Patteson refused; there was too much to do. On 27 April 1871 he set out on what was to be his last voyage among the islands of the Pacific. It was not the cheerful expedition that some of the earlier tours had been, for almost everywhere he went he found that the blackbirders had been before him. At Whitsuntide Island many men had been carried off by a "thief ship"; almost every man had been taken from Merlav; it was estimated that almost half the population over the age of ten had been kidnapped from the Banks Islands; in the Floridas Patteson was told that fifty islanders had been lured on board a vessel, ostensibly to trade, and had all been carried off to Queensland. Europeans on the same ship had dropped stones into the canoes surrounding it and then dragged the natives out of the water and took them to the sugarfields.

There were occasional bright spots on his tour. At Mota, for example, he baptised 248 men and women. But always the labour traders had cast their ominous shadows ahead. The Bishop saw three blackbirding vessels at Ambryn, three more at Mae and four at Santa Maria. The islanders no longer came down to the beaches to welcome their "bishopi". The word had gone out among the islands — the white men were coming to rob and kill. There seemed to be only one answer: the islanders would have to kill as well. The talking drums began to thunder out the fight-talk message.

On 21 September 1871, some time before eleven o'clock in the morning, the mission ship *Southern Cross* approached the island of Nukapu in the Eastern Solomons. On board were Bishop Patteson, Joseph Atkin, a New Zealand missionary, the crew, and a number of Melanesian boys being taken to the school at Norfolk Island. That morning Patteson had been teaching some of the schoolboys on the ship, reading them the story of the martyrdom of Stephen, concluding by saying: "We are all Christians here on this ship. Any one of us might be asked to give up his life for God, just as Stephen was in the Bible. This might happen to any one of us, to you or to me. It might happen today."

At 11.30 a.m. the ship's boat was lowered. In it were the Bishop, Joseph Atkin, Stephen Taroniara from Arosi on San Cristobal, and John Nonons and James Minipa, both from Mota in the Banks Islands. The small boat pulled for the reef where six canoes were waiting for them. When the boat reached the reef the tide was out and as it was impossible to row to the shore, Bishop Patteson transferred to a canoe and was taken to the beach, while the others waited for him just outside the reef.

Three canoes approached the ship's boat and the occupants asked the men from the mission ship where they came from. The

"The body of Bishop Patteson, murdered by the islanders, set adrift in a canoe". From *Cannibal cargoes*, by Hector Holthouse, 1969.

missionaries replied that they came from New Zealand, Bauro (San Cristobal), and Mota. At this the canoes began to drift away. Suddenly the men of Nukapu discharged arrows at the men in the boat, shouting as they did so, "This for New Zealand man!"; "This for Bauro man!"; "This for Mota man!".

The arrows tore into three of the four men in the boat! Stephen received six wounds, Joseph Atkin one, and John one. Only James, who had thrown himself into the bottom of the boat, escaped unhurt. In spite of their injuries the four men managed to row back to the *Southern Cross,* where they were helped on board by the horrified crew and schoolboys. Then they all turned their attention to the shore, wondering what had happened to the Bishop.

By that time John Coleridge Patteson was dead. On the shore he had been met by the chief of Nukapu, Moto. On a previous visit Patteson had befriended Moto, even to the extent of exchanging names with him: but now things had changed. Blackbirders had visited the islands of the Eastern Solomons. Five boys from Nukapu had been seized and taken to Fiji by a slave-trader impersonating the Bishop. Teandule, the uncle of one of the boys, had vowed to kill the first white man who landed at Nukapu. When Patteson came ashore, Moto conducted him to the shelter of a canoe house and had gone off, as he claimed, to prepare food for his distinguished visitor, leaving the Bishop with one small boy and Teandule. Patteson had lain down on the floor to rest. Teandule had approached him from the right-hand side, carrying a wooden club used for beating *tapa* cloth, and struck the Bishop on the side of the head, killing him.

On the *Southern Cross* Atkin, though fatally wounded, insisted on going back in the ship's boat to look for Bishop Patteson. Some of the schoolboys volunteered to go with him. Joseph Wate, a fifteen-year-old Malaita youth, and Charles Sapi of Ngela showed great courage in accompanying the missionary. Also on board were Charles Lapinamba, a sailor, and Mr Bongarde, the mate, who carried a pistol; it was the first time that a member of the crew of the *Southern Cross* had gone ashore armed.

Meanwhile, many of the island people were horrified at what had occurred. The women washed the body of the Bishop and

prepared it for a funeral. The men made five wounds on the
body and placed on the breast a palm with five fronds knotted,
to show that one life had been taken for five of theirs. The
islanders had wanted to bury Patteson in their own cemetery
some distance along the shore. The body was placed in a canoe
and a woman called Liufai got into a second canoe and began
to tow Patteson towards the cemetery. Then she saw the ship's
boat being rowed towards her and taking fright, let go of the
canoe she was towing.

The boat's crew secured the canoe and the body and took it
back to the *Southern Cross*. The next day, St Matthew's Day,
Joseph Atkin performed the burial service and John Coleridge
Patteson, first Bishop of Melanesia, was buried at sea. Also,
Joseph Atkin and Stephen Taroniara died as a result of their
wounds.

The death of Patteson caused a furore in Britain and the
Bishop drew forth a eulogy from Queen Victoria herself. There
was a marked increase in the number of volunteers coming forward
to serve as missionaries in the Pacific. The following year the
Government passed the Kidnapping Act to provide some sort of
justice for islanders sold into slavery. By his death Bishop Patteson
drew attention to the blackbirding trade, but it was to be many
more years before it ended.

8

THE NOBLE ARMY OF MARTYRS

Bishop Patteson was not the first Christian missionary to be martyred in the Pacific, nor was he to be the last. Even during the last thirty years of the nineteenth century, by which time some law and order had been imposed on the area, a number of missionaries were killed in the course of their work.

A particularly dangerous region was New Guinea which, together with New Britain, New Ireland, and other islands, lay to the extreme west of the sphere of influence of the Pacific missionaries. The first to visit had been the Marists who had established a mission on Woodlark Island in 1847, two years after the murder of Bishop Epalle in the neighbouring Solomons. It was not until 1848 that the Catholics moved on to mainland New Guinea. One small party under Bishop Collomb, Epalle's successor, built its headquarters on Rooke Island off New Britain, from which it was hoped to launch missionary expeditions to New Guinea itself. The scheme did not work. The area proved too unhealthy for Europeans and the missionaries fell ill, and in July 1848 the Bishop died of a fever. He was nursed by Father Villein, the priest who had ministered to Bishop Epalle just before his death: Villein himself died a few months later and the remaining Catholics abandoned their outpost and returned to Woodlark Island.

For four more years the Marists struggled to establish a foothold in New Guinea, with little success. In 1852 they were replaced by a group of missionaries from Milan, who fared little better, seeing one of their own priests, Father Mazzuconi, murdered on Woodlark Island before they too left in 1855. It was to be almost thirty years before the Catholics returned to New Guinea, and even longer before they again sought to establish missions in the Solomons. In 1882 Father Navarre, a Frenchman who became Archbishop of Papua, established the Sacred Heart Mission on Matupi Island, and laboured with great enthusiasm until the first Bishop, Father Couppe, was appointed in 1889. Seven years later the Mission of the Holy Ghost was set up by Father Eberhard Limbrock who built the first Catholic mission house on mainland New Guinea.

The Methodists also travelled towards New Guinea, sending a mission to New Britain and New Ireland in 1875 under the supervision of the Rev. George Brown. The mission ship *John Wesley* left Sydney for New Britain by way of Fiji, Samoa, and Rotuma. At Fiji an appeal was broadcast for native teachers to accompany the expedition, and there was a good response: Brown, a conscientious man, was careful to explain the hazards, but was still able to secure five married men and three bachelors. The authorities at Fiji were a little dubious; New Guinea at that time was almost completely unknown territory and its people had a reputation for ferocity in excess even of that possessed by the Solomon Islanders. The native assistants signed a document declaring that they were aware of the dangers of mission work in New Britain and New Ireland and that they were going there of their own free will. Two more native teachers, together with their wives, joined the expedition at Samoa.

The ship arrived at New Britain on 14 August 1875 and was at once surrounded by many canoes carrying excited natives. Some of the missionaries ventured ashore and almost at once walked into an intertribal skirmish; they withdrew with some speed. A mission station was opened at Nodup, not far from the present site of Rabaul, and a few hardy pioneers were sent over to New Ireland. The Methodists then began to branch out in various directions but it was not long before disaster struck: near Blanche Bay, a Fijian minister and three Fijian teachers were slaughtered and eaten. The instigator of the massacre was a chief called Talili who, up to that time, had possessed a monopoly of trade with the inland tribes. When Talili saw that the newly-arrived missionaries were already beginning to move towards the interior, he was afraid that they might start trading with the villages there, a not unreasonable supposition in the light of current mission practice in the Pacific. Talili thereupon led a band of tribesmen against the missionaries, killing three in the initial attack. One of the Fijians managed to escape but fled towards Talili, for some reason imagining him to be a friend: Talili cut him down.

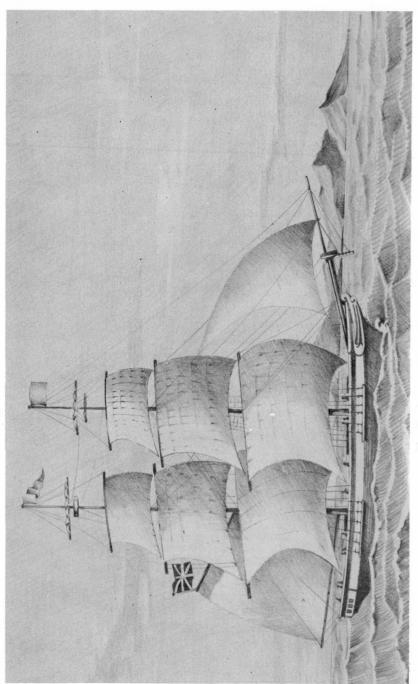

The Wesleyan mission ship *John Wesley*.

Brown was horrified: immediately he hired a leaky boat and with a band of Fijians and a few local guides penetrated the mangrove swamps and dense undergrowth overhanging the rivers, and managed to rescue the wives and children of the murdered Fijians. Some of the rescue party came into contact with Talili, finding him unrepentant, even boastful, and promising that he would kill every foreigner who entered his territory. Brown then came to a decision which was to whip up a storm of controversy. He decided that the missionaries must either teach Talili and his followers a severe lesson, or abandon the New Guinea mission. After a great deal of thought and prayer he issued muskets to the other missionaries and enlisted the help of at least one European planter. He was prompted by the determination of his Fijian followers to exact retribution for the death of their fellow-country-men: if he did not associate himself with the punitive expedition, the missionary reasoned, he would lose control of the mission altogether.

Accordingly a force of about sixty armed men moved into the jungle in search of Talili and his men. It must have been a bizarre expedition, the men of God marching through the steaming undergrowth, burning villages in their path and destroying banana plantations thought to be the property of Talili and his followers. Talili's men launched several attacks but Brown's men managed to beat them off. For most of this period Brown himself remained apart from the main body, trying to persuade other villagers to remain neutral. In the running battle with the missionary force several natives were killed. Talili escaped but his followers gave themselves up, agreeing to pay the missionaries native money in compensation and also handing over some of the bones of the murdered Fijian missionaries.

Brown's action in taking the law into his own hands received a great deal of publicity all over the world, and there was talk of trying him for manslaughter. But investigations conducted by naval officers despatched to the area concluded that he had acted for the safety of the people for whom he was responsible and should not be blamed. The Germans, who were taking a great interest in New Guinea, actually thanked him for protecting their trading interests.

The missionary remained in New Guinea only a few more

The Rev. George Brown, DD, and "natives" at Murua, New Guinea: from *George Brown, DD*, an autobiography, Hodder & Stoughton, London, 1908.

years. His time there was not a happy one: two of his children died in the territory and the local men and women proved largely indifferent to the message of Christianity propagated by the Methodists. Soon after Brown's departure three white men were shot only a few miles from mission headquarters, and the Europeans in the district launched another expedition against the tribesmen. It was not an area in which Christianity made easy progress.

The Lutheran Mission, which was established in New Guinea in 1886, got off to a better start when an epidemic was contained largely as a result of the skill and vaccines of some of its medical missionaries. This led to the Lutherans being tolerated, though it was not until the closing years of the century that they made their first converts.

The London Missionary Society was also active in New Guinea. The Rev. A. W. Murray and the Rev. S. MacFarlane brought a number of native teachers to the area in 1871. They had a rough time but persevered, the students from the college at Rarotonga being particularly effective in this new field of missionary endeavour.

Missionaries also established themselves in the Gilberts. In 1852 a vessel bearing American missionaries from Hawaii called in there. The Americans were surprised to find a number of European traders already in residence and doing quite well out of the coconut oil trade. A Union Jack flew over a trading post and there was generally a settled air to the islands which made them appear a desirable area for evangelising. Five years later the Hawaiian Evangelical Mission sent the Rev. H. Bingham, the son of the pioneer missionary in Hawaii, to open a station in the Gilberts.

Bingham and the others were fortunate in that a leading European trader there, Richard Randell, was interested in Christianity and even before the arrival of the missionaries had courted death at the hands of the islanders by deliberately breaking local *taboos* and preaching the word of God. The trader was kind to the missionaries and Bingham, who appears to have been a fine and effective leader, wrote:

Captain Randell still gives pleasing and increasing evidence of a determination to find the pearl of great price. At a recent visit to Apaiang, he again showed his kindness to us by a present of 20 sovereigns. He now purposes dissolving partnership with Capts Smith and Fairclough after the present year, and looks forward to a life somewhat similar, I may say, to that of Paul's, the making known the Gospel to the Kingsmill Islanders at his own expense. He proposes to leave off trading in tobacco, as he has also left off smoking it, and to sell useful articles to the people of this group, while he is desirous of doing good to those from whom he has acquired his property, which now probably exceeds $25,000.

Randell was a little over-ambitious in his declarations, but he was of considerable help, even if he did not prove to be a latter-day Paul. Later the London Missionary Society landed Samoan teachers, and in 1888 two priests and a lay brother of the Catholic Sacred Heart Mission landed as the result of an invitation from a French trader and some Gilbertese men who had returned from the plantations of Tahiti, where they had embraced the Catholic faith.

The different religious denominations proved puzzling to the Gilbertese, especially as the relationships between the Europeans of the different missions were far from harmonious. One traveller in the South Seas, Frank Burnett, described a scene in which a native chief called Tanoa approached the Deputy Commissioner in the Gilberts and asked him in pidgin what kind of God belonged to the white man that so many different people told the Gilbertese different things about Him:

You know, Mr. Cogswell, me like smoke tabac very much, me also want very much to go to heaven. Mr Walkup, you know him, he big man Boston Mission. He come along and say "Suppose Kanaka smoke tabac he go hell." He say "You savvy great big shark, man-eating shark. Well, much more easy big shark go through needle, what you call him, eye of needle, than man who smoke tabac, he go heaven." So I say I no smoke tabac, and I b'long Boston Mission. By 'm by, Mr. Goward, he chief London Mission, come island. He told big meeting in Maneappa and preach. He say plenty good men smoke tabac go heaven, suppose smoke tabac he no go hell. I want smoke very much, I say "All right, I b'long London Mission." After Mr. Goward go, I walk along beach by Catholic Mission. Father Phillip he come out and call "Ai-yah, Tanoa. Why for you not come along Catholic Church?" I tellim what Mr. Walkup say, what Mr. Goward say. He laugh very much. He say all Protestants go hell, only Catholics go heaven. Now, Mr. Cogswell, what kind of a God you white man have, and which fellow he tell me big damn lie?

By the end of the nineteenth century most of the missions in the Pacific were training native preachers. In Samoa in particular there were several training schools and colleges. William Churchward described the Marist church and college at Apia in 1887:

The Mission owns a large quantity of land about Apia, devoted chiefly to food cultivation, worked by the catechists. On the hill immediately in rear at Vaea stand their college and another church, approached through a fine avenue of tall native trees; whilst judiciously scattered around are to be seen many useful trees and plants, introduced by these good people for the benefit of those to whom their lives are devoted.

He went on to give an account of the London Mission's headquarters at Malua:

Here are always in residence some fifty or sixty Samoan students, training for teachers and missionaries. When qualified, which takes a course of four years, they are either set to work at home in Samoa, or sent to the different islands of the Pacific whenever required to assist in the good work.

At this time the London Missionary Society was having its share of trouble with its Samoan students. There was a strong movement afoot to send all European missionaries home, the students pointing out with some truth that it was the native teachers and missionaries who were sent to the dangerous and unpleasant areas while the majority of European mission workers occupied safe administrative positions. The move to oust the Europeans failed, but it caused a great deal of agonised heart-searching while it lasted. Another thorn in the flesh of the LMS was the behaviour of one or two isolated Samoan teachers who seemed to have a less than perfect understanding of their true function. For example, one ex-student of Malua who was sent to the Ellice Islands promptly annexed the group, hoisting the Samoan flag and taxing and fining the inhabitants before he was hastily removed from office.

It was on Tonga that one of the most unusual and intriguing passages of mission history was conducted in the closing decades of the nineteenth century. It was almost a throwback to the early days of the first missionaries and their "missionary-kingdoms" in the Pacific. The man responsible was a Methodist called Shirley Waldemar Baker, who became one of the most important and influential white men in the South Pacific. Baker was born in Gloucestershire in 1835 and emigrated to Australia when he was eighteen. For a time he studied pharmacy and then entered the Wesleyan ministry. In 1860, when he was twenty-five, Baker was sent as a missionary to Tonga. The island had then been ruled for fifteen years by the enormous and powerful (in every sense of the words) King George Tubou. His reign, which continued until 1893, when he was ninety-six, was successful for the Tongans, despite the vicissitudes caused by the feuding missions and the occasional interference of inquisitive and acquisitive European powers. By 1862, when he had subdued the warring minor chiefs of Tonga, Tubou was even ready to draw up a constitution. This he did at the urging of the Methodist

The Rev. Shirley Baker.
From an engraving in the
Alexander Turnbull Library,
Wellington.

King George Tubou I
of Tonga.
Courtesy of the
Dixson Library, Sydney.

missionaries who had been impressed by the recent emancipation of Hawaii. Under Tobou's constitution all Tongans were to be subject to the law of the land, irrespective of rank; chiefs were no longer to levy money or derive forced labour; officials were to be appointed and paid; there was to be a Parliament.

The missionaries were pleased with their part in the new constitution and regarded with an indulgent eye the resultant feast, which began at Nuku'alofa on 4 July 1862 and continued for two months, during which time 150,000 yams and 9,000 pigs were eaten.

It has been claimed by his adherents that Shirley Baker drafted the 1862 constitution, but if he did it was almost certainly in committee with the other Methodist missionaries on Tonga. There is no doubt, however, that he was quickly becoming the most important and influential missionary in the Friendly Islands. An ambitious and energetic man, he was also a vigorous and fiery preacher, and his church meetings were always well attended. He was also a man of wide interests and varied talents. Before he had been on Tonga more than a few years he had designed a national flag, interested himself in a system of roads and, so it was claimed, been offered the post of Prime Minister by King Tubou, an offer that was rejected on this occasion. By 1870 Baker was the leading missionary and the king's right-hand man. Tubou was too strong and independent a character to become a puppet, but he realised that in his kingdom's increasing dealings with Australian and European authorities the help and advice of a shrewd white man would be of considerable use.

Among Baker's talents was the ability to raise money for the Tongan mission — in fact by 1874 the Tongan Methodist Church was self-supporting. Tubou asked that Baker's employer, the Australian Wesleyan Board of Missions, allow the Church in Tonga to become self-supporting and self-governing, and that it should stop diverting its funds to Australia. The request was promptly refused, to the annoyance of the Tongans. It also provided a black mark for Baker in Australia, where he was suspected of having put the king up to the proposal.

His next move was in the political field. In 1876, on behalf of the king, he negotiated a treaty with Germany by which that nation recognised the independence of Tonga and the sovereignty

King George's palace, Tonga, where the Rev. Shirley Baker and his family took refuge during some troubles on the island. An engraving in the Alexander Turnbull Library, Wellington.

of Tubou. In exchange Germany received certain trading rights and the use of the harbour of Vava'u as a coaling station. The treaty was signed on a visiting German man-of-war by the German Consul-General from Samoa and the ship's captain, with Baker acting for Tubou. At the last moment Baker did some shrewd horse-trading without reference to the king, ensuring that the coaling station remained Tongan property. The Germans were satisfied and even bestowed a decoration on the missionary for his part in its implementation. But the treaty caused some alarm in Britain, it being regarded as another instance of German interference in British spheres of influence, and Baker was castigated for his part in the matter. A British official visited the Friendly Islands. His worst fears were confirmed when the king declared that Baker had indeed been influencing him against Britain, insisting that the British wished to swallow up Tonga in the newly-created Western Pacific High Commission. This in fact had been mooted by the Foreign Office, and Baker's obduracy over the independence of the Friendly Islands did nothing to endear him to the British Government, especially when Britain had to be content with a treaty signed in 1879, which merely gave British traders some concessions and in return insisted on Tongan independence.

By this time Baker's religious and political power was obvious to all. The Australian Board of Missions investigated the Tongan Church in 1879 and declared itself thoroughly dissatisfied with his conduct. At almost the same time Sir Arthur Gordon, a British official, complained that Baker had far too much power over Tubou, being regarded by the monarch as a combination of adviser, banker and doctor. The Australian Methodists attempted to remedy the situation at its Conference by ordering the missionary to return to Australia. Baker resigned from the mission and was appointed Prime Minister by King George Tubou.

Now he had the trappings of power and was not slow to use his influence. In 1882 he drew up a Declaration of Rights, approved by the king. Three years later he showed his contempt for the Australian Board by setting up the Free Wesleyan Church of Tonga. The British High Commissioner in the Western Pacific advocated deporting him, but it would have caused too much unrest. As was pointed out, if Baker should be deported the king would be greatly upset and might well take a German as his Prime Minister, in which case the British would have jumped out of the frying pan into the fire.

Having cast himself adrift from the Church authorities in Australia, Baker proceeded to discourage the Tongans from remaining loyal to the Wesleyans and to encourage them to join his Free Church. He paid his ministers higher salaries than the Australians could manage, and ordered his police force to use whatever methods they could to misuse and annoy the Wesleyan ministers and missionaries. Schools were taken over from the missions by the state. By this time Tubou was very old and regarded as increasingly under Baker's thumb. The former missionary took more and more power unto himself, spent much of his time travelling to Australia and New Zealand, and employed European secretaries and bodyguards.

The Tongans who remained loyal to the Wesleyan Church were discriminated against, particularly those in vulnerable positions in public service, the militia, and at college. Some two hundred Wesleyans, including the daughter of the king, were deported to Fiji and to the uninhabited islands of Tofua and Tonumea. Some Wesleyans took refuge with the British Vice-Consul, who informed the Western Pacific High Commissioner what was happening.

There was an attempt on Baker's life, attributed to the Wesleyans but in reality the work of four escaped convicts, who fired at the Prime Minister as he rode past in a carriage. They missed him but wounded his son and daughter who were also in the carriage. The event was the cue for another purge of religious adversaries on the part of the now autocratic Baker. He brought in armed mercenaries from Ha'apai and Vava'u to harry the Wesleyans.

At this juncture Sir Charles Mitchell, the British High Commissioner, arrived, aghast at the stories he had heard from the Tongans forced to flee to Fiji. Mitchell investigated Baker's activities and concluded that the Prime Minister had acted in a tyrannical manner, but conceded that the king deemed his services indispensable. Mitchell had to be content with securing a promise of complete religious toleration throughout the kingdom from King George Tubou.

Baker was subdued for a while, but it was not long before he was again doing all in his power to make life unpleasant for those who had the temerity to oppose or attempt to thwart him. He even went so far as to publish a document stating that all the troubles in Tonga were the result of British interference. The authorities had been waiting for the Prime Minister to make a false move, and Sir John Thurston, Mitchell's successor as High Commissioner in the Western Pacific, forced him to withdraw his accusations and to apologise. The British Government was still apprehensive about annoying Baker, but Thurston had no such scruples. Baker's administration in Tonga was proving inefficient as well as despotic, taxes were crippling the people, yet official salaries were not paid, and there was a great deal of discontent.

In 1890 Thurston visited Tonga and told the king that the promises made to Sir Charles Mitchell had not been kept and that Shirley Baker was no longer a person acceptable to Her Majesty's Government as Prime Minister of Tonga. Tobou, now over ninety, did not greet this declaration with the fire and indignation it might once have received. A letter was sent to Baker, dismissing him from all his official posts and giving him twelve days to leave Tonga. Baker blustered and argued but Thurston was adamant. Her Majesty's ship *Rapid* was in harbour as a potent argument. Baker accordingly spent a night burning official papers then obediently left the Friendly Islands. Some years later he returned and even worked as a missionary again, this time for the Church of England, but by then King George Tubou was dead, his great-grandson ruled in his place, and had no time for the once all-powerful Prime. Minister. Baker lingered on, a nuisance to some, but never again regained the position that had once been his.

By the end of the century the Wesleyans, the Free Methodists, the Anglicans, and the Catholics were in Tonga, all disliking each other intensely and competing for the souls of the Tongans.

Shirley Baker was not the only missionary in the Pacific in the closing decades of the nineteenth century to become deeply involved in politics. The Presbyterians in the New Hebrides, particularly the influential John G. Paton, were loud in their denunciations of the increasing French interest in the region. The New Hebridians seemed fated to be robbed or exploited in one way or another: after the excesses of the sandalwood traders and the blackbirders, the planters moved in to clear thousands of acres and plant cocoa and coffee and cultivate coconuts: and the French in New Caledonia. were particularly interested in the commercial prospects of the New Hebrides and began to move in in some force.

Led by Paton, the Presbyterians created an enormous fuss in Australia and Britain, pointing out that where the French were established, Catholicism flourished. Eventually, after much argument, the New Hebrides became an Anglo-French Condominium in 1906, but if it had not been for the storm whipped up by Paton in 1877, it is possible that the New Hebrides might have become a French possession in the nineteenth century.

The missionaries were often the only white men in the New Hebrides who were not there to exploit or rob the natives, but even the Presbyterians had their problems. When there were over twenty-five white missionaries among the islands by 1880, Paton

Dr John G. Paton. Frontispiece to *John G. Paton: later years and farewell,* by A. K. Langridge & F. H. L. Paton, London, 1910.

had to fend off criticism that his missions were overstaffed. His reply was dignified and effective, and during the course of it he gave a thoughtful description of the technique of evangelising an area:

We plant down our European Missionary with his staff at a given Station. We surround him with Native Teachers, who pioneer amongst all the Villages within reach. His lifework is to win that Island, or that People, for God and Civilization. He masters their Language, and reduces it to writing. He translates and prints portions of the Bible. He opens Schools, and begins teaching the whole population. He opens a Communicants' Class, and trains his most hopeful Converts for full membership in the Church. And there he holds the fort, and toils, and prays, till the Gospel of Jesus has not only been preached to every creature whom he can reach, but also reduced to practice in the new habits and the new religious and social life of the Community.

The Catholics sent missionaries to the New Hebrides during this period. In 1887 four Marist priests and a number of New

Mission chapel at Maré or Nengoné, Loyalty Islands. From *Gems from the Coral Islands, Volume I,* by the Rev. William Gill, Ward & Co., London, 1856.

Caledonian lay brothers were distributed among the islands. Another wave of Marists hit the Banks Islands, hitherto a stronghold of the Melanesian Mission famed for its village of Mota and the great banyan tree Bishop Patteson called his cathedral. It is impossible to tell how successful these different missions were in Melanesia. Each faith claimed its converts, but there were many lapses and backslidings and even among those islanders who claimed to be Christians there were many who understood little about the religion the white men had brought to them.

While the majority of missionaries in the South Pacific towards the end of the century were sober and conscientious men, and there were few colourful characters of the type found among the earlier men of God in the South Seas, at least one flamboyant self-styled missionary flourished. His name was Walter Murray Gibson, an American who became a naturalised Hawaiian citizen. Among other things he was a Mormon who tried to persuade Brigham Young to sell Utah to the United States Government and move all his Mormons to New Guinea. When this idea failed he did his best to unite most of the Pacific islands into a gigantic federation, narrowly avoided a lynching party, and died a millionaire.

Gibson, like many of those strange idealistic rogues who found a spiritual home in the Pacific in the nineteenth century, seems to have had the ability to convince himself that his more hair-raising schemes were perfectly logical and proper. The son of English migrants, Gibson claimed to have spent much of his youth with a tribe of Indians. He joined in the California goldrush and for a time was a soldier of fortune in Central America. He is next heard of captaining a decrepit schooner in the gun-running trade, surviving a mutiny, and being concerned in some unspecified manner with the death of a number of his crew in a brawl before sailing the vessel for Sumatra in the Dutch East Indies. Here Gibson became involved again in his old trade of arms smuggling and was clapped in jail at Java by the Dutch authorities. Gibson, a glib, engaging scoundrel, languished in prison for over a year, an embarrassment to his captors, who feared reprisals from the United States but were loathe to release him.

Eventually Gibson escaped, probably with the connivance of the Dutch, made his way back to the United States, published a best-selling account of his adventures, sued the Dutch for $100,000, failed in his claim, and was appointed to an official post at the American Legation in Paris. He did not stay long before returning to the United States about 1859, where he offered himself to the Latter Day Saints, or Mormons, and was appointed a missionary to the Pacific. In 1861 Gibson arrived at Hawaii where for some reason he did not at once announce himself as a missionary and was suspected by some of being a Confederate spy, the Civil War having broken out in the States.

Later Gibson began work as a missionary, becoming the leader of the Mormon Church on the island of Maui and spreading his activities to a number of other small islands in the area. At this juncture he appears to have begun entertaining thoughts of building his own particular New Jerusalem on the island of Lanai, where earlier Mormons had decided to establish a mission. Gibson gave himself the imposing title of "Priest of Melchizedek and Chief President of the Isles of the Sea" and gathered funds for his earthly paradise by selling official positions to all comers. The islanders were not quite as naive as Gibson would have hoped, and a complaint to Mormon headquarters brought an official committee hurrying to Lanai. A quick but comprehensive investigation revealed that the mission leader had been doing well out of the business transactions he had been conducting in the namē of the church, and that the mission land was now officially Gibson's property.

The Mormons wasted no time in excommunicating him and he reluctantly turned from affairs of the spirit to more temporal matters. Over the next twenty years he became in turn a labour agent, newspaper owner in Hawaii, politician, privy councillor, land speculator, and finally cabinet minister in the country he had adopted. A grandiose scheme to form a confederation of island states with Hawaii at its head failed, and an effort to take over Samoa incurred the wrath of Germany and had him scuttling back to the safety of Hawaii where he was almost lynched when he became involved in a riot. Eventually he returned to the USA, where he died peacefully in 1888.

The Mormon Church continued to do a great deal of effective work in the Hawaiian islands and later built its own headquarters on one of them, along the lines of the establishment originally planned by Gibson. The leaders of the Latter Day Saints must have been relieved to have dispensed with the services of their missionary relatively early in his career: but they were probably a little surprised that this curious man did not fulfil the prophecy of one Mormon leader, that Gibson would die in the gutter.

Considering the prestige of the missionaries in the Pacific it is surprising that so few rogues and vagabonds attempted to use the cloak of the Church for their nefarious ends. People like Gibson were very few; the overwhelming majority of missionaries in the South Seas were hard-working and dedicated men and women, always striving to extend the boundaries of their work. By the end of the nineteenth century they had landed in every island group and introduced some form of pastoral care to every large island in the Pacific. They had even extended as far as the Solomons, hitherto the least known and most savage island group. After the death of Patteson the Anglican Melanesian Mission continued its work, the Catholics returned, and two new denominations, the Methodists and the South Sea Evangelical Mission, started to evangelise areas of the Solomons. Both arrived within a relatively short time of each other.

The Methodists first landed in the Western Solomons in 1902, having been invited by islanders who had become converted to Methodist Christianity while working in the Queensland sugar-fields. On their return to the Solomons some of these men, mainly from the islands of Malaita and Guadalcanal, had written to the Wesleyans. This was a genuine case of the mission being invited in, but the Methodist authorities were a little dubious because of their agreement not to trespass on Melanesian Mission territory. However the Rev. Dr Brown, who had first taken Methodism to New Guinea, visited the Western Solomons in 1899 and saw that the Anglican missionaries had not touched that area and that the people seemed willing to accept a Methodist mission. Brown recommended that it be opened in the Roviana area, as the people there were the most powerful in the west, and feared and respected by the other Solomon Islanders. If these men and women could be converted, declared Brown, the other tribes and groups would soon fall into line.

On Friday, 23 May 1902, Dr Brown arrived with the Revs. J. F. Goldie and S. R. Rooney, Mr J. R. Martin, four Fijian teachers, two Samoans, a New Hebridian and one Solomon Islander who had been converted in Fiji. Mission headquarters were set up at Munda. Goldie, a generous, hard-working, and extremely practical man, emerged as the mission leader. He was a down-to-earth character who amassed a considerable private fortune by dealing in land in Australasia and the Solomons, and used this money to help his mission work. The presence of a mission worker who could afford to pay for things instead of the customary poverty-stricken Church representative, impressed the Solomon Islanders. Goldie believed that everyone should work as hard as he did, saying:

> I am convinced that mission work amongst savage people, if it is to succeed, must be on industrial lines. I hope that I shall not be misunderstood when I say that, with the exception of the white beach-comber, who has sunk below the level of the natives on whom he sponges, is the religious loafer. The loafer is at all times objectionable, but the half-civilised native who loves to strut round quoting passages of the Bible, singing

The Rev. J. F. Goldie and Solomon Island chiefs.

hymns, and shaking hands on the slightest provocation, but who has learned nothing of industry, honesty or cleanliness, is the most objectionable of all. He is a by-product of Christian missions. He has been taught a Christian creed divorced from Christian conduct. He is to be pitied more than blamed.

Goldie's long tenure of office and driving personality did much to ensure the growth of Christianity in the Western Solomons, but the real impetus to spreading the faith was provided as usual by the native teachers. These Fijians, Samoans, and Tongans did not live apart from the Solomon Islanders as the white men tended to. They lived in the villages and shared the lives of the islanders. The two Tongans Paul Havea and Vili Hopoate were particularly respected. Such men had a great influence on the people of Roviana and the surrounding districts, and not only in the sphere of religion. Some aspects of the culture of the native teachers were assimilated by the islanders and are part of the lives of the people of the Western Solomons to this day. The islanders adopted the small outrigger canoes introduced by the Tongans, and copied their superior methods of gardening and food cultivation. The weaving methods of the Samoans were

Some Kanaka labourers decided to stay on in Queensland and after their time expired; they would build homes like the ones above.

incorporated by the women of the district and the distinctive Western Solomons mats of today were copied from those of the first Samoan teachers. Songs and games of the other islands were also taken over by the admiring people of Roviana. Other denominations notably the Catholics, came to the Western Solomons, but Methodism has remained the paramount faith there throughout the twentieth century.

In 1904 the South Sea Evangelical Mission, then known as the Queensland Kanaka Mission, came to the Solomons. This denomination, like the Methodists, owed its presence there to the island labourers working in the Queensland sugar plantations. The established churches did little to cater for the plantation workers and their spiritual welfare was looked after in the main by individual ministers and small evangelistic societies.

One such mission worker was Florence Young, a member of the Plymouth Brethren, who first began ministering to the Pacific islanders in 1882 on a Queensland estate owned by her brothers. Three years later the first native convert was baptised, an event that gave Miss Young great satisfaction and led to her forming the Queensland Kanaka Mission as an undenominational evangelical mission, one of several in Australia at that time.

Miss Young left for missionary work in China in 1890 but the QKM continued its work. Though the labour trade was to be brought to an end and most of the islanders repatriated at the end of the first decade of the twentieth century, towards the end of the nineteenth century the islanders in their thousands were still being imported into Australia, particularly from the Solomons. Miss Young returned in 1900 to direct the work of the mission and to come to grips with the problem of organising some kind of follow-up work to that being done by the QKM in Australia. Normally converts were delivered into the hands of a suitable Protestant mission on their return to their home islands, but with the many Solomon Islanders this was not an easy matter. The Anglicans of the Melanesian Mission were not yet particularly widespread in the Solomons, and in any event were suspected of being rather High Church in their attitude. That left only the Catholics at the turn of the century, and the thought of turning over any of their converts to them was anathema to Miss Young and her fellow workers.

There seemed but one logical course to follow — QKM would have to establish a mission in the Solomon Islands. Miss Young's determination was strengthened by a series of messages from one of her converts, Peter Ambuofa, who had returned to his home on Malaita and was trying to work as a missionary on his own. He had obtained a number of converts, though his teaching was by no means orthodox and was sometimes horribly confused. The Melanesian Mission had attempted to help Ambuofa but he wanted no assistance from that quarter: he wanted the QKM to come to the Solomons to finish what they had started.

In 1904 the mission decided to take the plunge and Miss Young led a party which included A. Hedley Abbott, James Caulfield, and O. C. Thomas. The British administrator was a little dubious about the new arrivals, for Malaita was notoriously a restless area and considered dangerous for Europeans. (A few years later Jack London visited the island and described it, perhaps with some exaggeration, as "as near the rawest edge of screaming savagery as any place on earth".) Miss Young was adamant. She and her fellow missionaries settled in the Malu'u district, the area previously evangelised in part by Peter Ambuofa. Within a short period Miss Young contracted malaria and was forced to return to Australia, but came back to the Solomons in 1905 and settled down to the task of establishing mission stations. In 1907, by which time she and her colleagues were making some progress, the name of her organisation was changed to the South Sea Evangelical Mission.

Towards the end of the nineteenth century Christianity was well established in the eastern and central parts of the South Pacific, but in the west the missionaries had to struggle for every convert, and this was particularly true of New Guinea. After the episode in 1875 in which Dr Brown reluctantly agreed to a punitive expedition against the murderers of some of his teachers, the missionaries of all faiths found progress very slow indeed. The London Missionary Society had sent its first representatives to the area in 1871 when the Rev. S. Macfarlane, Mr Murray and eight native teachers landed on an island in the Gulf of Papua. Other missionaries, both European and native, followed. By this time, though originally it had been interdenominational, the LMS was mainly Congregational.

One of its leading missionaries in the early days in New Guinea was James Chalmers who arrived after service in Rarotonga and spent some twenty years in the Pacific. Like many of his kind he was an explorer as well as a missionary. He established friendly relations with several natives but his work was always fraught with danger. In 1881 eight native teachers were murdered at Kalo in Hood Bay and Chalmers accompanied the punitive expedition to see that there was no unnecessary bloodshed. He wrote:

I was on the coast at the time, and was sent for; and on the day after my arrival the flagship Wolverine came into Port Moresby with Commodore Wilson,(later Rear-Admiral Wilson, on board. He came to the Mission House and asked me to accompany him, as he had determined to make war on Kalo, secure the chief, the real instigator of the crime, and hang him. I objected; but he said my accompanying him would make his mission one of peace, and he should be sorry if a single shot was fired.

The Commodore was a little optimistic in hoping for a bloodless expedition, but though there was a sharp battle Chalmers's presence ensured that there was no looting and that the local women and children were saved.

Chalmers and the Rev. W. G. Lawes were the outstanding LMS missionaries in New Guinea in the closing decades of the nineteenth century. It was Lawes who was entrusted with the task of interpreting to the local chiefs at the ceremony declaring New Guinea a British protectorate in 1884. Chalmers continued to

The London Missionary Society's Church at Aird Hills, about 300 miles north-west of Port Moresby. The mission was established in 1913; twelve years earlier, the Rev. James Chalmers and his companions were murdered by a neighbouring tribe.

press farther into the interior but in 1901 he and a fellow missionary were attacked from behind, killed, and later eaten.

In 1891 the first Anglican missionaries arrived in New Guinea. For some time previously the Church in Australia had been considering opening a mission: at the General Synod in 1886, the Bishop of North Queensland had moved:

> That the recent annexation of a portion of New Guinea imposes direct obligation upon the Church to provide for the spiritual welfare, both of the natives and the settlers. That, as the Mission should be conducted on an adequate scale and provision made for considerable outlay, its expenses should be shared by all dioceses in Australia.

Five years later the pioneers of the mission made the journey, under the Rev. Albert Maclaren. The Anglicans had chosen wisely — he was to be a fine first priest. His adventurous life had started almost at his birth, for his parents were sailing for the Falkland Islands when the vessel encountered bad weather, and Mrs Maclaren insisted on being put ashore at the Isle of Wight, where she gave birth to Albert. The ship, sailing on, sank at sea. He entered the ministry, serving at first in a slum parish in Britain. Believing he had received a call to overseas mission work, he persisted in his applications despite rejection because of his delicate health, and was eventually accepted. He served in several Australian parishes where he established a reputation for persistence and courage, and then in 1887 sailed back to England as a companion to the invalid Bishop Pearson. He spent a year working for a degree at Durham, his expenses paid by his former parish in Queensland, and when his studies were completed, offered himself for missionary work to the Society for the Propagation of the Gospel. He was accepted and returned to North Queensland, before taking up work in New Guinea. During 1890 he made two exploratory visits to New Guinea; on one of them he was called on to minister to the survivors of the steamer *Quetta*, which had struck a rock and foundered. Maclaren did what he could but with a flash of opportunism on behalf of his mission also wrote to the Queensland newspapers, suggesting that a fund be raised to build a memorial church to those who had perished, the church to be built on Thursday Island in the

Torres Strait. The idea caught on, about £2,000 was raised and the church erected.

It was during one of these visits that he met Sir William MacGregor, the Governor of New Guinea and a man deeply sympathetic to the missions and their workers. They took to each other, Maclaren writing of the Governor:

British New Guinea is to be envied in having such a man as Sir William MacGregor as its Administrator. His whole life is spent in studying the natives, and endeavouring to understand their peculiarities. Already he has gained a marvellous influence over them, and they recognise him as the Big Chief of New Guinea. He is also deeply interested in missionary work, and I feel sure that we shall have in him one who will do all in his power to help us.

Maclaren's high regard was reciprocated. During his first visits the missionary showed the Governor that he was a sensible and adaptable man who would not cause unnecessary strife. MacGregor was particularly impressed by the way in which Maclaren set out to establish friendly relations with the missionaries of other denominations already there, for Maclaren realised that men like the LMS minister Lawes, Brown of the Methodists and Bishop Verjus of the Catholics could give him a great deal of help and advice.

When Maclaren arrived to take up his work in 1891, he was already a tired man. For seven months beforehand he had stumped up and down the Australian continent arousing interest in the New Guinea mission and attempting to raise funds and secure volunteer helpers. He made one particularly good catch in a young man called Copland King who was to be one of New Guinea's most effective mission workers. King agreed to accompany Maclaren to New Guinea and the two of them, together with three carpenters and a native guide and interpreter, finally went ashore at Dogura, the site suggested for their mission station by Sir William MacGregor, on 13 August. After some on-the-spot haggling, the Anglicans bought the land from the local chief for ten tomahawks, ten big knives, ten small knives, twenty-five pipes, thirty pounds of tobacco, five shirts, some cloth and a few beads.

Some European lay workers arrived soon afterwards but there were some early blows: Copland King became ill and had to return temporarily to Australia; and building proved so difficult under the conditions of heat and constant rain that the carpenters were sent home. Even Maclaren became depressed by the lack of all-round progress. It was during this period that he allowed himself one of his rare moments of despondency in a letter:

Don't think that I wish to complain, but after all, I am only human and I am fond of pleasant people and social life. Here, then, I shall be for three years, and then, if God spares me, a change, perhaps for good, as by that time the Mission will need another head than mine to manage affairs. I hope that you remember me in your prayers for I am sure that I need them. Pray that we may be kept free from fever and other troubles in New Guinea.

While the building of the mission station was being completed by native labourers, Maclaren found time to make a number of journeys into the neighbouring countryside. He did his best to make peace between two feuding villages and spent many days travelling on foot between them. Inevitably his health began to go; he collapsed and was carried on board a ship. On 27 December he died: his mission had lasted a little over four months.

Copland King, who had been recuperating in Australia, was appointed the new head of the mission and left to join the few lay workers remaining, arriving in April 1892. King was an Australian, a quiet, contemplative man. Some may have had doubts about his suitability to lead a mission in such a primitive area as New Guinea, but he soon showed that his tenure was to be no mere holding operation. Within a month he was cruising in a small boat, looking for a location for a second mission. He carried on Maclaren's avowed policy of collaborating wherever possible with the other missions. In 1893 there was a conference with the LMS and the Wesleyans at which a number of recommendations were made to the authorities regarding local marriage customs. At this meeting agreement was reached that all three missions would refer to Jesus as *Jesu Keriso* in their dealings with the natives.

King established schools and learned the local Wedauan tongue, translating hymns, psalms, reading books, and part of the Prayer Book. He obtained a mission schooner, the *Albert Maclaren,* and sailed along the coast for considerable distances. In 1896 he performed his first baptisms in New Guinea — there was two local candidates and King gave an account of the simple ceremony:

I took Aigeri by the hand, led him into the water, and as he stood there I poured water on his forehead and baptized him Samuela, and having been signed with the sign of the cross, he stepped up into the assembly of Christians; and then we did the same for Agadabi, and Pilipo was added to the Church.

More than once King was invited to become the first Bishop of New Guinea, but he refused. In 1897 Montagu John Stone-Wigg was nominated for the post, King indicating his willingness to serve as second-in-command. More expatriate priests were volunteering to come and serve in the area. By the end of the nineteenth century, though years of work lay ahead of all the Churches in New Guinea, Christianity was definitely established there.

9

A WORK OF TIME AND MUCH LABOUR

Throughout the nineteenth century the missions of all faiths in the South Pacific were too far from their parent bodies in Europe to depend on them for immediate succour and support in time of adversity. Communications were unreliable and painfully slow, so that by the time an answer to a particular problem arrived from mission headquarters, the problem had usually been solved or had changed its complexion radically. Thus it was to the newly-established colonial settlements in Australia and later New Zealand that the South Seas missionaries began to look for aid and comfort. A number of the pioneers of the LMS fled from Tahiti to Port Jackson in New South Wales at the end of the eighteenth century when the Society Islands became too unruly, and for many years afterwards the new settlement was used as a base and refuge for Pacific islands missionaries.

In addition to using Australia and New Zealand as springboards for South Seas ventures, the Churches were naturally concerned with ministering to the colonists and engaging in evangelistic campaigns among the indigenous inhabitants of both countries. It would not be possible here to give a comprehensive account of the progress of the different denominations in Australia and New Zealand throughout the nineteenth century; brief mention of the establishment of Christianity and its contact with the natives will have to suffice.

Though Captain Cook had landed at Botany Bay in 1770, it was to be eighteen more years before settlers arrived in New South Wales. With the loss of her colonies in the American War of Independence, Britain had to find a new penal colony for her lawbreakers, and the area discovered by Cook was decided on as suitable. Some people thought that Botany Bay would be too dreadful even for convicted lawbreakers. One newspaper declared:

> The eastern coast of New Holland is, perhaps, the most
> barren, least inhabited, and worst cultivated country in the

southern hemisphere; and Botany Bay is at too great a distance from any European settlement to receive either succour or friendly assistance.

Even so the colony was adopted as the scene for a convict settlement. Captain Arthur Phillip was brought out of half-pay retirement, put in charge of the expedition and announced as the first Governor of New South Wales. On 3 May 1787 he sailed for Australia in charge of a fleet of eleven ships carrying about 1,500 people, over half of whom were convicts, both men and women. There were some extremely rough customers among them, but there were also some convicted for offences which would be regarded today as less than serious, or not even offences at all. This has been summed up by Sydney Smith:

> One man is transported for stealing three hams and a pot of sausages; and in the next berth to him on board the transport is a young surgeon, who has been engaged in the mutiny at the Nore; the third man is for extorting money; the fourth was in a respectable situation in life at the time of the Irish Rebellion, and was so illread in history as to imagine that Ireland had been illtreated by England, and so bad a reasoner as to suppose that nine Catholics ought not to pay tithes to one Protestant. Then comes a man who sets his house on fire to cheat the Phoenix Office; and lastly, that most glaring of all human villains, a poacher driven from Europe, wife and child, by thirty Lords of Manors, at the Quarter Sessions, for killing a partridge.

Other penal convoys followed; the conditions on some vessels were tolerable but on most they were bad, but it was on them that some of the convicts came into contact with missionaries. None went to New South Wales in the first years of the settlement's life, but a few of them took passage on vessels in the fleet and left when the ships touched at Africa to carry out evangelistic work in that continent. While they were on board they did their best to help the prisoners. One such missionary, a member of the LMS, described the conditions and the work he and his colleagues carried out:

> But our brethren were not only preaching and teaching, but subjected to the painful and dangerous employment of reaching the hospital, and attending the dying beds of those who were

The Rev. Richard Johnson, first chaplain in Australia. From the *Illustrated History of Methodism, Volume I*, by James Colwell, William Brookes & Co. Ltd, Sydney, 1904.

now sorely afflicted with a putrid and pestilential fever, a misery which hardly any convict ship escapes, considering the persons who come aboard from jails and hulks, and the place where they are confined in irons; the dreary darkness of which, the closeness, the heat and putrid effluvia, are inconceivable to those who have not visited these abodes of wretchedness, and with the clank of the chains, affords the strongest idea of Hell, and of the damned, which can be conceived. Disease now advanced with rapid strides, and death began to make havoc among the convicts. Our intrepid brethren intermitted none of their friendly offices, but visited the hospital, and stood over the beds of the dying, exposed to all the danger of so dreadfully infectious a situation, and earnestly employed in endeavouring to pluck those brands from the burning.

On arrival at the settlement, which Phillip moved from Botany Bay to Port Jackson, the prisoners and their guards set about building a camp. From the beginning life was hard and discipline tough. The settlers had to support themselves, and the succeeding fleets of prisoners. The story of the early years of the colony is of desperate endeavour, disease, and disappointment. Some of the convicts tried to escape; a few succeeded and took to the bush or even sailed to Pacific islands; most died or were recaptured and flogged. Slowly the colonists made progress, but life was never easy.

There was little interest in spiritual matters in the settlement, yet the one clergyman did his best for his unusual flock. He was the Rev. Richard Johnson, chaplain to the First Fleet, a compassionate, conscientious man but lacking, it would appear, fire and personality. He conducted the first church service in the open soon after the arrival of the fleet. It was plain that neither the exiled prisoners nor the marines were interested in the message Johnson was trying to bring them. This did not prevent him from doing his best. During one of the epidemics that swept the colony in 1790, a young man wrote home, saying:

I believe few of the sick would recover if it was not for the kindness of the Reverend Mr. Johnson, whose assistance out of his own stores makes him the physician both of soul and body.

On the whole the officials seemed to regard Johnson as of use mainly on formal church-parade functions. On 9 June 1790 it was recorded:

Being the day appointed for returning thanks to Almighty God for his Majesty's happy restoration to health, the attendance on divine service was very full. A sermon on the occasion was preached by the Reverend Mr. Johnson who took his text from the Book of Proverbs: "By me kings reign".

Johnson did his best against the odds and even found time to engage in pioneer farming but he seems to have been a relatively insignificant figure in the colony. More convicts arrived but little food. Smallpox broke out among the Aborigines. Norfolk Island was chosen as a penal settlement for the more incorrigible convicts. The Rev. Richard Johnson became disillusioned and wrote to Governor Phillip:

There is another thing which I beg leave to relate to your Excellency, and that is the matter in which the holy Sabbath is observed. I have often lamented, and not seldom complained, of the thinness of the congregation, sometimes not one half, one third, and sometimes one fourth of the convicts (especially the women) present. Many of the officers, both civil and military, and I may add of the naval and merchant line too, have frequently apologised for their non-attendance, and have assigned as the cause the want of a convenient place of worship.

We have been here now above four Years, and the first time we had public service in Port Jackson I found things more comfortable for myself and for the congregation (for whom I would ever feel as for myself in such circumstances) than I did last Sunday, for then we had the advantage of the trees to shelter us from the Sun; but now we were wholly exposed to the weather, first to the rain, which I was fearful would have made me dismiss the people, and afterwards to the wind and sun. On this account, Sir, it cannot be wondered at that persons, whether of higher or lower rank, came so seldom and so reluctantly to public worship. I have, not seldom, found very great inconveniences attending it myself. . . .

I neither wish or mean to interfere with any thing that does not concern myself; but as the Clergyman of the Colony, and as intrusted with the spiritual charge of those unhappy people, and us, I submit it to your Excellency's own consideration whether before the approaching winter, some place should not thought of and built both here and at the new settlement for the purpose of carrying on public worship.

Johnson received scant sympathy from Phillip who, in that same year, sailed for England on sick-leave and then resigned the governorship, going on to a quietly distinguished if belated climb to the rank of Admiral. Johnson had to fend for himself. The following year after his letter of complaint (1793) he built his own church in the New South Wales colony. It was constructed of wooden posts, wattle, and plaster, and covered with thatch. Unfortunately it was to have a short life. Some of the prisoners, annoyed at being forced to attend services on pain of suffering fifty lashes if they abstained, burned the building to the ground in 1798. Another church was built in its place and attendance every Sunday enforced among the convicts by special constables.

Under Phillip a little exploration had been undertaken, mainly in search of better agricultural land, and this was found near Parramatta. For most of Phillip's tenure of office the colonists were too busy cultivating land and getting their food from the soil to have much time for voyages of discovery, especially as most of them were convicts under close guard as they worked. After Phillip's departure there were two temporary governors,

The first church in Australia, built by the Rev. Richard Johnson. From *A Century of the English Church in New South Wales,* by E. C. Rowland, Angus & Robertson, Sydney, 1948. Original drawing in the Mitchell Library, Sydney.

each a military member of the New South Wales Corps. Not unnaturally a military elite began to grow up and by the time Governor John Hunter arrived in 1795 he found the officers of the corps busily engaged in private commerce under the leadership of John Macarthur, an officer in the New South Wales Corps, a quick-tempered, quarrelsome man who had built up an enormous amount of power in the colony and considered himself the equal of any governor sent out from England.

While Macarthur and his fellow officers did their best to make life difficult for Hunter, the Rev. Richard Johnson, overworked, disillusioned, and increasingly peevish, continued to go about his parish work. In addition to the spiritual needs of his congregation he was responsible for the education of the many children in the colony, and he established several schools, using at least one convict as a tutor and wrote constantly to England asking for more teachers. He was also well aware of the needs of the Aborigines, though understandably he seems to have washed his hands of them as one of his responsibilities. As early as 1792 he was writing home:

I hope in time that these ignorant and benighted heathens

will be capable of receiving instruction, but this must be a work of time and much labour. It would be advisable and is much to be wished that some suitable missionary (two would be better) was sent out for that purpose.

The Aborigines, their land taken by the colonists, their women prostituted, their tribal customs falling into abeyance before the new culture, hunted for sport by white men in some regions, were certainly in need of help. In thirty years in the area of Sydney alone their numbers fell from an estimated 1,500 to several hundred. It was a pattern repeated throughout Australia as the free settlers who followed the convicts began to occupy and farm the land that had once been the hunting grounds of the natives.

When help did come from the missions, it was mostly too late and often of the wrong kind. As numbers dwindled, missionaries admitted that there were not enough indigines left to make it worth setting up missions. By the 1830s Count Strzelecki, visiting Australia, wrote of the Aborigines:

Degraded, subdued, confused, awkward and distrustful, ill concealing emotions of anger, scorn or revenge, emaciated and covered with filthy rags; these native lords of the soil, more like spectres of the past than living men, are dragging on a melancholy existence to a yet more melancholy doom.

Richard Johnson had no way of foreseeing the fate of the Aborigines when he made his plea for missionaries. He was having more than enough trouble with the Europeans in the colony. He and his sole colleague, the Rev. Mr Bain, chaplain to the New South Wales Corps, who pioneered evangelistic work on Norfolk Island, 800 miles from the coast of Australia, were finding that discipline and good order, never strong, were becoming less and less effective. John Macarthur and Governor Hunter were engaged in a vicious feud. They were making accusation and counter-accusation to the authorities back in England, who were not very interested in the penal colony at the other end of the world. In one letter Hunter throws light on some of the abuses with which Johnson and Bain had to put up with when trying to carry out their duty among the drunken soldiers and convicts. Hunter is replying to an accusation labelled at him by Macarthur:

His observation relative to the vice and profligacy of the

The "Missionary Window" in the church of St John the Evangelist, Toorak, Victoria, features an Australian Aborigine. Above his head are the stars of the Southern Cross, and his boomerang is at his feet.

lower orders of the people I will agree in the truth of, and your Grace will recollect how much I have said upon it in my public correspondence. But let me ask him, under whose authority were the people suffer'd to indulge in licentiousness, drunkenness, and every abombinable act of dissipation? When the clergy were allowed to be insulted in the streets without receiving any kind of redress, and rendered incapable of performing the dutys of their sacred office on the Sabbath Day, from the numbers of drunken soldiers and convicts surrounding the outside of the place of public worship, and often engaged in card-playing and riot; let me ask this pretended advocate for the moral conduct of the people, what were his answers to the clergyman when he complained to him of such shamefull and unpardonable excesses, and on the spot, too, where his duty lay, and where he commanded?

While the administrators bickered and the soldiers and convicts roistered, another clergyman arrived in New South Wales, to work at Parramatta. This was Samuel Marsden, stocky, stern, and tactless, destined to become one of the most effective and controversial ministers in the early years in Australia and New Zealand. Marsden was born in 1765 in Yorkshire, where his father was a small farmer and blacksmith. His early years were unadventurous; the first twenty being spent in the village of his birth. Then came a sudden spurt — Marsden plainly was a late developer. After two years as a probationer of the Elland Clerical Society he went to Hull Grammar School and from there to Magdalene Hall, Cambridge. He did not stay to take a degree, but in 1793 was ordained, and he accepted the post of assistant chaplain to the convict settlement in New South Wales.

From the start it could be seen that Marsden was a man to be reckoned with. Men of the cloth were not regarded highly in New South Wales but the new chaplain showed that he was not the ineffectual idealist some had anticipated. Well-organised and uncompromising, Marsden was also just. He trod on toes and made enemies. He also did a great deal of useful work. He cultivated and developed a model farm, using his agricultural background for the purpose, and helped to sustain a number of missions and schools. His talents were not long in being recognised. The London Missionary Society asked him to become its

representative in Australia. He proved a tower of strength to the
Pacific missionaries during their initial struggle in Tahiti. By 1800,
when Johnson left, he was the senior chaplain in New South
Wales. Governor Hunter made him a magistrate, though the
chaplain's uncompromising attitude later led to his being dismissed
from the bench and not reinstated for some years. Marsden was
not the stereotyped parson of fiction. For a time he undertook the
duties of superintendent of public works; where his strictness made
him few friends. He was hardly less lenient on the bench and
certainly not averse to ordering flogging as a punishment.

He made no attempt to disguise his low opinion of the moral
character of many members of the colony. In a report written
in 1806 he said:

> It is to be lamented that since its commencement to the
> present time there has scarcely appeared a germ of virtue on
> which to build a hope of the general character changing for
> the better. The depravity and vice which pervades a large portion
> of the community does, by its preponderating influence, effect
> the whole, and gives to the individual habits and manners much
> to be deplored. Any attentive, humane observer, who might
> visit the colony, would soon be convinced of the truth of these
> remarks; and when he beheld a rising generation of several
> hundreds of fine children exposed to a contamination fatal to
> body and soul, he would tremble for their danger.

The colonists found Marsden much tougher-minded than the
departed Richard Johnson. He was unconventional and resource-
ful. When the new senior chaplain discovered Henry Fulton, a
political prisoner from Ireland, who was also an ordained minister
among the convicts, Marsden secured the use of his services as
an assistant. He was less liberal with the Roman Catholic priests
among the Irish prisoners, but he could be little else: authority
would have nothing to do with that religion in the colony. There
had been Roman Catholics among the very first prisoners to come
to the settlement in New South Wales, but there was no freedom
of worship in the early days. Catholics were forced to attend
Protestant services and were flogged if they did not. When Roman
Catholic priests deported from Ireland began to arrive, the
authorities were in a predicament; and this deepened when several
Roman Catholic priests arrived as chaplains on convict ships in

1798. Mass was celebrated in the early years of the nineteenth century, but when one priest, Father Jeremiah Flynn, arrived without permission, the Governor had him deported. For some years the faith was forced to go underground. One former convict, William Davis, an Irishman, secreted in his cottage a Sacrament consecrated by Father Flynn before his enforced departure. It was not until 1820 that two Roman Catholic priests, Fathers Therry and Connoly, were allowed by the British Government to found a Church in Australia. Fourteen years later Bishop Polding became the first Catholic Bishop in Australia.

The Church of England had an equally desperate time in establishing itself, in spite of the efforts of Marsden and his colleagues. Governor Hunter left the colony in 1800, his authority undermined by Macarthur and his fellow-officers in the New South Wales Corps, to be replaced by Philip Gidley King. King found Macarthur too well entrenched to make much headway against him, and for the six years he governed New South Wales he was in conflict with the other man. King, however, was the first governor to attempt to do something about the increasing lawlessness of the Pacific islands, and particularly the depredations of the white men who exploited the area. For once he found himself at one with Macarthur, who asked the Governor to rescue trade in the islands "from the hands of foreigners, or from men, whose loose and immoral characters threaten to produce the most fatal effects upon the rising generation".

There was little that Governor King could do to exercise jurisdiction over the scattered and remote Pacific but he did demand bonds of good behaviour from masters of vessels leaving New South Wales for the islands, and also appointed men of known good character in the Pacific as Justices of the Peace, including the Rev. John Jefferson at Tahiti. That was about as much as King could do, beset as he was by Macarthur, who was probably the richest and most influential landowner in the territory. King withstood the attack until 1806 and then abandoned the struggle and was replaced by yet another Governor — Bligh of *Bounty* fame.

Bligh was not a man to be bullied. He and Macarthur collided head-on almost from the start, leading to the well-named "Rum Rebellion", one of the most bizarre episodes in Australia's history,

during which Bligh was arrested by members of the militia under
Major Johnstone, commander of the New South Wales Regiment,
who claimed to have received a letter signed by Macarthur and
others informing him that it was his duty to depose the Governor.
Johnstone himself gave an account of the letter:

> In a short time after, a letter was presented to me imploring
> me instantly to put Governor Bligh in Arrest, and to assume
> the Command of the Colony. The letter was also approved by
> all the Officers of the Corps present at Head Quarters: and as
> the events I had myself witnessed left me no cause to doubt
> the propriety and necessity of complying with this requisition, I
> immediately ordered the Corps under Arms, and directed four
> Officers to proceed to Government House and summon
> Governor Bligh to resign his Authority.

Order was restored eventually. Bligh was reinstated in office
for a short token period of one day and then shipped home to
England. Johnstone was court-martialled and dismissed the service.
Macarthur, by now a civilian, was not brought to trial but was
not allowed to return to Australia from England until 1816. Lachlan
Macquarie, forty-eight years old, proud, remote, and autocratic,
came out to govern the colony, bringing with him a strong military
detachment under Colonel O'Connell. For the first time the
settlement was to be ruled by a really firm hand.

Macquarie was willing enough to help the established Church
of England in the colony, but found that there was little enthusiasm
among his senior colleagues. In 1812 the Governor was persuaded
that Sydney should have a cathedral. After four years of delay
one of the convicts, a former architect named Greenway, drew
up plans for what he called Greenway's Metropolitan Church,
St Andrews. These plans included provision for ornamental
gardens, a bishop's palace, a divinity school, museum and library.
In 1817 Governor Macquarie laid the foundation stone of the
cathedral. Work on the building had hardly got under way when
Commissioner Bigge stepped in with a diatribe against the folly
and expense of such a needless luxury. Anyone could see that
the first requirement of the town was another prison, not a
church! Accordingly work on the cathedral stopped and it was
some decades before it was finally built.

Marsden was not slow in reminding Governor Macquarie of

St Matthew's Church, Windsor, 35 miles north-west of Sydney. Consecrated in 1822, St Matthew's is one of three churches designed by the convict architect Francis Greenway (1777-1837).

his responsibility to the Pacific islanders, particularly in guarding them against the excesses of Europeans in the area. In 1813 the senior chaplain had founded the New South Wales Society for Affording Protection to the Natives of the South Sea Islands, and Promoting their Civilisation. Macquarie did his best to afford what protection he could, accepting that the wellbeing of the islanders could be supervised only from Sydney, but his resources were not sufficient to allow him to do much practical work towards clearing undesirable Europeans out of the Pacific, nor even to apprehend and bring to trial the more brazen among their number.

Mission societies of different faiths were beginning to come to Australia and venture into the Pacific, and they joined in protesting against the activities of some of the traders. The missionaries and the traders had the area much to themselves. The only obligation of the British Government was to protect the Australian colony against any attack; it did not seek to extend its influence far into the Pacific. It is only fair to add that the missionaries did not want the authorities to colonise the Pacific islands. They feared that any such colonisation, as in Africa, would result in hordes of undesirable Europeans streaming into the area, undermining the work of the missions.

In New South Wales itself other denominations had joined the Anglicans and were establishing churches. The Anglicans were given the status of an arch-deaconry under the Bishop of Calcutta in 1825 and in the following year the Rev. Thomas Scott was appointed the first archdeacon. In 1836 William Broughton, who followed Scott as archdeacon, was consecrated Bishop of New South Wales under the authority of the Archbishop of Canterbury.

The Rev. Samuel Leigh, the first Methodist missionary, arrived in 1815; Methodist teaching had begun in Sydney three years earlier when two schoolmasters, Thomas Bowden and John Hosking, led the first class meeting. Presbyterians had held services during the early days of the settlement; their first church was built in 1809 at Ebenezer in New South Wales, and the first Presbyterian minister, the Rev. Archibald McArthur, arrived in Hobart in 1822. One of the most prominent among the Presbyterians was Dr John Dunmore Lang, who as a minister, politician, and newspaper proprietor, fought and railed against injustice and intolerance wherever he encountered it in the colony.

In 1831 the Baptist Church under the Rev. James McKaeg began its work in Sydney, a year after the Rev. F. Miller had held the first Congregational church service in Hobart. In 1846 the Church of Christ built its first Australian church in Adelaide.

During the first fifty years of the colony's existence men had been pushing its borders farther and farther back. In 1802-3 Matthew Flinders circumnavigated the continent, and in 1813 Gregory Blaxland, William Lawson and William Wentworth were the first to cross the Blue Mountains and open the way to the rich pastures of the Bathurst region and fresh expansion by the early settlers. George Evans discovered and explored the Macquarie River, and other pioneer farmers advanced as far as the plains around Goulburn. Other explorers blazed new trails — Hamilton Hume and William Hovell, Allan Cunningham, Charles Sturt, and others. The crossings of unknown land populated by frightened and antagonistic Aborigines were sometimes fatal. Ludwig Leichhardt was lost attempting to cross the continent from east to west, Edmund Kennedy was murdered while exploring Cape York, Burke and Wills died on their way back to Melbourne from the Gulf of Carpentaria.

After the explorers came the settlers, and the settlers were followed by the missionaries. As we have seen, there was all too little for the missionaries to accomplish among the Aborigines. Chased from their hunting grounds, subject to new diseases, increasingly bewildered and dispirited, the indigines were soon a dying race.

By the middle of the century the Churches were turning increasingly to parochial problems among the white settlers. The most important of their joint activities lay in the field of education. At first all education was in the hands of the various denominations. While some schools were good, the system was not. Rivalry between the denominations led to too many schools in one area and not enough in another. Education in Australia was not compulsory and large numbers of children never went to school at all. Different governors appealed to the Churches to settle their disputes and arrive at some comprehensive and generally agreed system of education, but the rivalry between the Protestants and the Catholics was too great to allow of a compromise for some years.

In 1844 a committee appointed to study the problem discovered that only half the children in the colony were receiving any education at all. It was obvious that something would have to be done, and the state introduced the so-called Irish system of education, which was designed to run in tandem with the church system, both forms being supported by the state. It was a compromise, and though not particularly happy, it was the best that could be devised under the circumstances. At least it saw the colony entering the second half of the nineteenth century with a rather more comprehensive system of education than before.

The first missionaries to reach New Zealand did so in 1814, brought to the country by the bustling Samuel Marsden. For some years this clergyman had wanted to spread his wings and see the Anglican Church established through the whole of Australasia. He had first secured volunteers for the pioneer work in New Zealand as early as 1807, though he had to wait seven more years before he could introduce the missionaries to their new sphere of activity. At the time, and for some years afterwards, New Zealand was an extremely wild area. The first Europeans to visit in any numbers were sealers, whalers and other seafaring men, who put in for water or supplies of the timber which grew so freely. They encountered the Maoris — bigger, fiercer, more advanced than the Aborigines of Australia — and traded with them, exchanging pork and vegetables for knives, axes and muskets. The latter were particularly prized and used in intertribal warfare.

The first white men to settle were deserters from ships and escaped convicts from New South Wales. Most of them seem to have been accepted by the Maoris and used as advisers, particularly on warfare and fighting tactics, by leaders of different tribes. When the first missionaries arrived the Maoris saw that they were men of a markedly different stamp. Marsden had planned his campaign with some care; he had talked a great deal with Maoris who had visited Australia, and had convinced the Church Missionary Society that the country was ripe for conversion.

Marsden and his companions landed at the Bay of Islands on 22 December 1814. The senior chaplain preached the first sermon,

"Samuel Marsden's first service in New Zealand." A painting by Russell Clarke, reproduced in *Holly Leaves*, Christmas number of the Illustrated *Sporting and Dramatic News*, 1946.

based on the text "Behold, I bring you glad tidings of great joy". He then left the other missionaries to do what they could and returned to Australia, though he maintained a watching brief on the Church in New Zealand and visited the country again and again throughout the rest of his life.

Other missionaries followed, some ordained, others laymen, craftsmen like the first LMS missionaries in the Pacific. The early days of the Anglican mission were not easy and not all the missionaries were equal to the gigantic task. The numbers of Europeans in New Zealand were increasing, trade in flax and kauri timber was developed, and whalers set up more than twenty bases in the country. The Bay of Islands, where the missionaries had established their headquarters, became a popular trading centre. Relationships between individual Anglican missionaries were not always amicable, and there was more than a little petty squabbling.

Governor Macquarie welcomed the restraining influence of the missionaries in neighbouring New Zealand and in the first year of their arrival appointed one of them, Thomas Kendall, Justice of the Peace at the Bay of Islands, with responsibility for the protection of the Maoris against European traders; one of Kendall's new duties was to see that no sailor was discharged from a British ship in New Zealand without the permission of one of the major chiefs.

Having the missionaries in New Zealand, however, was to prove a mixed blessing, for in 1817 Governor Macquarie received a strongly-worded letter from the London headquarters of the Church Missionary Society. It complained that the Europeans in New Zealand were committing atrocities — so much so that the missionaries were unable to get near the indigines. Another letter from the society, this time to Earl Bathurst, went so far as to say that it might prove necessary to withdraw the CMS missionaries from the Bay of Islands and even from other Pacific islands unless the Government found some way of punishing European offenders, either in New South Wales or Britain.

Bowing to such spirited and influential pressure, the British Government passed an Act of Parliament providing for the punishment of serious offences in the Pacific committed by British subjects. It was a vague and not completely satisfactory piece of legislation, and Britain remained too far from the South Seas to be able to enforce it in any great detail, but it was a start. No matter how small the beginning, law and order were being brought to bear on the Pacific, thanks largely to the work of a missionary society.

The first missionaries in New Zealand were interesting men and presented the usual cross-section of humanity. Thomas Kendall, one of the first to work in the Bay of Islands, proved a student both of the Maoris and their language. He took two Maori leaders to Britain on one of his periods of leave, but it was not a happy experiment as one of them seemed more concerned with ordering supplies of firearms than in appreciating "civilisation". On his return Kendall embarked on a study of Maori beliefs and traditions, the better, he claimed, to be able to refute them and bring home the benefits of Christianity to the people. Unhappily he appears to have become a little too interested and involved in Maori life, and in particular their women, resulting in a tirade from Samuel Marsden and the dismissal of Kendall. The latter lived with the Maoris for a time and was next heard of as a clergyman in Valparaiso; he died in Australia. Poor Kendall, he meant so well and was one of the few missionaries to attempt to understand the Maoris. In a way this was probably his undoing. In what could almost have been his epitaph, he said, "I have been so poisoned by the apparent sublimity of their ideas that I have almost completely turned from a Christian to a heathen."

Another man suspended from the Church by Marsden, and for much the same reason, was William Colenso, the mission printer who published parts of the New Testament in the Maori tongue. Colenso remained in New Zealand, a productive and influential citizen, even becoming for a short time a member of the parliament of the rapidly developing country.

The affairs of the mission had become chaotic when Henry Williams, a former naval officer, now an ordained clergyman, arrived in 1823. Some of his naval officer's mannerisms remained with the new missionary, but his occasionally domineering attitude was forgiven by those who recognised that here was a man capable of putting the mission's house in order. This he did, aided by such shining lights among the early missionaries in New Zealand as his brother, William Williams, and Octavius Hadfield, both of

Archdeacon Henry Williams and his brother, William Williams, are approached by a group of Maoris threatening to destroy Henry Williams's potato crop. From *Illustrations of Missionary Scenes, Vol. II*, 1856.

whom later became bishops. Hadfield was an outstanding Christian who took his faith to the Maoris and stood by them throughout their troubles with the Europeans.

In 1822 the Rev. Samuel Leigh, who had first brought Methodism to Australia, established a mission at the Bay of Islands, near where there had been a massacre of white men in 1809. The Wesleyans were forced to move after a time because of trouble between different tribes of Maoris, and established a fresh mission on the west coast's Hokianga harbour. The Anglicans and Methodists co-existed peacefully until the arrival of Bishop Selwyn. Selwyn, less Low-Church than his colleagues in New Zealand, was not as amenable to the Wesleyan Methodists as Williams and the others.

By 1830 European influence was making itself felt. A group of businessmen formed the New Zealand Association to colonise the country and establish trade with the outside world. Decent settlers came out to join the convicts and deserters who had found their way there. During the 1830s there were a thousand white men and women in the country, and many more were to come. In 1840, after pressure from the Association, New Zealand was annexed for Great Britain by Captain William Hobson, the newly-appointed Lieutenant-Governor.

For all their influence, the missionaries had played a relatively minor part in the annexation. Over the years Samuel Marsden had made one or two tentative suggestions about settling desirable British subjects in the country, and had pointed out the trading advantages, particularly in timber, but the missionaries were not over-concerned with the problem, regarding it as political.

At the ceremony of annexation, however, the Church was well-represented. The Catholics, who had arrived in New Zealand in 1838, had their bishop in attendance, and a number of Anglican missionaries watched approvingly as their leader, Henry Williams, interpreted for the Governor as the terms of the Treaty of Waitangi were read out to the assembled Maoris. Williams must have had mixed feelings; he knew that both the Church Missionary Society and the Wesleyan Society had grave doubts about the advisability of colonising the country and opening the floodgates to all and sundry. The Directors of the CMS had made its position clear when the 1837 Report of the House of Commons Committee on Aborigines was being prepared: no more lands should be colonised, native peoples should be allowed to live in peace, subject only to the peaceful and beneficial ministrations of Church workers sent out for the purpose.

Such worries and doubts were mainly for the established Church of the land. Meanwhile, the Roman Catholics devoted all their energies to working among the indigines. Bishop Pompallier and his assistant, Father Louis Servant, had arrived at New Zealand after their voyage from Europe, during which they landed Marist Fathers and Brothers on various South Sea islands. The two Catholics set up their headquarters at Hokianga where they worked for two years before transferring their mission to Kororareka in the Bay of Islands.

Father Servant has been described by those who knew him as a gentle, kindly man, almost childlike in his simple faith. For four years he worked among the Maoris and in the midst of all his work found time to write to Father Colin in France, sending

him a complete account of his observations of the culture, customs and living conditions of the Maoris. In 1842 Father Servant was sent to the Pacific island of Futuna, where Father Chanel had been martyred, to spend thirteen years toiling in hardship and danger. After several years in Samoa his health failed and he was recalled by his superiors. He died in 1860.

Other priests came to New Zealand and worked among the people. Father Jean Baptiste Petitjean was one of the first, arriving in 1839 with four other missionaries. Celebrated for his intellect and quick tongue, he was chosen by his colleagues to play a prominent part in the famous debate held between Catholic priests and Protestant ministers before an audience of Maoris at Kororareka in October 1841. What the indigines could have made of a debate conducted at a furious pace in English is difficult to say, but both Protestants and Catholics seemed to have enjoyed the dispute and, needless to say, both parties claimed to have come off best.

Another early arrival among the Catholic priests was Father Antoine Garin. He showed great courage during tribal wars in the 1840s, trying to bring peace to the combatants and ministering to the hurt. In these early years the Catholics found themselves lacking in almost every material possession. A letter from Father Garin to Father Colin in 1842 gives some idea of the trials of the mission:

> Yesterday I· received news from nearly all the Fathers, those at Tauranga, Maketu, Matamata, Opotiki, Auckland and Hokianga. I tell you that after spending two hours reading the story of all the sufferings, corporal and spiritual, which burden our poor Fathers, I was unable to restrain my tears. . . . I sent twenty-five pounds sterling to Father Borjon, so that he, with Father Rozet and Brother Deodat might go to Port Nicholson, and these twenty-five pounds were stolen with several letters. Father Baty, so long expected at Kororareka, tells us at last that he is already in Auckland, and that he dares not come, for fear we may have nothing to pay his passage. Father Petit asks for several things. I am sending him today a little flour, some rice, some tea, etc., all bought on credit at Kororareka. . . . But these are not the most keenly felt trials. Our greatest cross is to see that we cannot go among the natives as often as we would wish, for want of a little tobacco — and above all, books. Our natives do not know how to hide their mortification when the Protestants say to them: "Here are our books, where are yours?" We spend all our time in copying.

The early days of the French Marists in New Zealand were far from easy. They were robbed of their one seaworthy boat, largely ignored, and in constant danger of death. Some of them were lost at sea. Throughout the tribal wars they continued to do what they could, gradually increasing in numbers and influence.

The Anglicans received an impetus in 1842 with the arrival of George Augustus Selwyn, the thirty-two-year-old first Bishop of New Zealand. Selwyn, like many of the most successful missionaries, was not an easy man to get on with, but a more popular bishop might have been less effective. From the first he proved that he was more than a mere administrator. His long-distance walks across New Zealand were to become famous, as were the controversies in which he became involved.

A dispute with Henry Williams to a large extent over land Williams had purchased, had resulted in the latter's dismissal; but in 1855 Selwyn was largely instrumental in persuading the Church

Missionary Society to reinstate Williams, though the whole confrontation could, with a little foresight, have been averted.

There was also Selwyn's distrust of the Methodists. Samuel Marsden had welcomed their arrival in New Zealand and the two denominations had got on well until Selwyn came. He, however, could not forget that they were Nonconformists. Though they had left the Church of England of their own free will, in Selwyn's opinion they were little better than laymen and had no authority to baptise the Maoris. He made no secret of his feelings and a rift opened rapidly between the two churches, which came to a head in a letter of protest from a Methodist missionary, the Rev. H. H. Turton, published in the New Zealand *Southern Cross*:

For the last twenty years there have been two churches in this country — the Episcopalian and the Wesleyan — using the same form of public worship, and in the administration of the sacrament, using the same Scriptures and Book of Common Prayer (the objectionable passages always excepted), preaching the same doctrines, and exercising the same system of moral discipline. The island has been divided into two compartments, so that no minister should interfere with the parish of another. . . . Members of the two churches, likewise, after the established custom of the mother country and for scriptural reasons, have been mutually admitted to partake together of the holy sacrament of the Lord's Supper. . . . It would appear from your lordship's directions to the natives of this district, that the utmost distance is, in future, to obtain between the two parties, — that separate services are to be established in the same village — that the attendants of one native hut are no longer to enter the threshold, or resort to the services of another native hut — that Wesleyan ministers are to be forbidden to preach in *such consecrated places* — that their ministrations are not to be attended by any but their own people; and that in some pas . . . *they are not to be allowed to preach the Gospel at all within the boundaries of the village fence* . . .

Selwyn's reply was temperate but firm: the Wesleyans had renounced the mother Church and were in a state of schism, and he could not recognise their missionaries as ordained ministers. He was sorry but that was all there was to it.

Certainly no one could accuse him of being undecided in his

views or of physical laziness. In 1842, together with Chief Justice Martin and some fifty natives to pole six canoes, he set off on an extensive journey along the eastern coast of North Island. Alternating between canoe voyages and overland marches they made the first recorded trip from Manawatu to Hawke's Bay, including following the path of a disused war track and crossing the Raukumara mountain range. Such a journey made by a Church dignitary, even one as young as Selwyn, attracted a great deal of attention outside New Zealand and he became the epitome of muscular Christianity for many, even to the extent of having the author Charles Kingsley dedicate his book *Westward Ho!* to him.

Mrs Selwyn sometimes accompanied her husband and has left an account of one of the journeys, giving a good idea of their mode of travel:

> We left Wellington for Waikanae, Mr Hadfield's post, on the west coast, in primitive style, George on foot, I mounted on Mr Hadfield's very nice horse accustomed to bush journeys; the two maids with one between them . . . little Willie in a large potato kete affixed to poles and carried by two men, and about four Maoris also on foot.

Bishop Selwyn was not of course the first missionary to explore hitherto undiscovered territory in New Zealand. From the very beginning the missionaries, a more potent force than they had been in New South Wales, were striking out in fresh directions. In 1814, before Samuel Marsden made his initial visit, Governor Macquarie had insisted on other missionaries going ahead to discover the lie of the land. Marsden was considered too valuable to be risked, especially as there was no guarantee of immunity for Christianity and its messengers now that Te Pahi, a chief who had earlier expressed interest in conversion, had been killed. Accordingly the others made an exploratory trip lasting some six weeks, living and sleeping among the Maoris. Only when they reported that all seemed well did Macquarie allow his senior chaplain to leave Sydney.

Once in New Zealand Marsden made up for lost time. After preaching his Christmas sermon in the Bay of Islands he arranged to travel thirty-five miles inland, the farthest so far attempted by Europeans, with the chief Hongi. At the beginning of 1815

"Passing through a swamp in New Zealand." From a Church Missionary Paper of 1836.

Marsden journeyed to the interior, getting as far as Lake Omapere before returning to the coast. Even then he was not content, but for a further six weeks cruised up and down the coast of the North Island, talking to chiefs and making arrangements to buy, for twelve axes, 200 acres of land on behalf of the Church Missionary Society. He left three missionaries behind him: Thomas Kendall, a schoolteacher, William Hall, a carpenter, and John King, a shoemaker.

For four years Marsden was immersed in church affairs in New South Wales but in 1819 had occasion to return to New Zealand to mediate over a dispute between the missionaries. He was pleased to hear that in spite of some dissension two missionaries, after an initial period in which they had not strayed far from the mission station, had managed to get as far overland as Hokianga. Marsden promptly gathered some companions and made the same journey, being greatly impressed with the beauty of the area.

In June 1820 he sailed along the coast of the North Island in the Royal Naval vessel *Coromandel,* leaving her at one point to go up the Firth of Thames and walk some distance inland. He returned to the ship, made a journey in her whaleboat to inspect space in the vicinity of the Waitemata, and returned once more to the *Coromandel.* Here the captain told the wandering missionary that he would have to return to the Bay of Islands by canoe as the vessel had no plans for putting in there. Marsden was far from averse to the project, but when some Maoris informed him that the weather would be too inclement for such a journey, he seized the opportunity to return by land, walking as far as possible and hiring canoes where he had to.

It was the beginning of one of the major early journeys undertaken on foot in the northern part of the North Island. In the course of it the indomitable clergyman and his companion crisscrossed the peninsula, venturing where no European had been before and making at least one major discovery, that of Maukau Harbour. No maps had been made of the terrain and the area was cut by swift rivers. The fact that Marsden could not swim did not deter him in the slightest, he merely made arrangements to be carried across the rivers in a hammock. Between February and October 1820 Marsden covered hundreds of miles, completing the journey and embarking for Sydney an exhausted but happy man.

For a few years after this epoch-making exploration the missionaries were unable to travel far into the interior. It was the era of vicious intertribal warfare, sometimes known as the Musket Wars because the Maoris were able to use firearms obtained from the Europeans. It had not been unknown for missionaries to trade in muskets with the natives, and this had been one of the reasons for the dismissal of the unhappy Kendall. The son of a missionary of this period later wrote about life in New Zealand during the Musket Wars:

> One of the first things I can remember at Tauranga was being taken by my father to see a fort which the Maoris were building under the direction of the missionaries as a place of refuge. It was close to our houses, and on the edge of a cliff. A wide and deep ditch was being dug, and the earth taken out of it formed into a wall. To prevent the soil, as it was being heaped up,

falling back into the ditch, alternate layers of fern and soil were placed one above the other. I was too young to realise that what I saw being done meant the approach of danger.

The guiding hand of Henry Williams was of great use to the mission during this period. He was not afraid to discard plans that would not work and he would have nothing to do with Marsden's idea of an agricultural economy for the New Zealand mission. It was the duty of the mission to convert, not feed itself, argued Williams, therefore the emphasis would be on evangelism.

This led to the missionaries beginning to venture forth again, at first cautiously but then with increasing confidence. In 1831 Williams took advantage of a peace he and Marsden had negotiated with the Maoris to travel as far as Rotorua, one of the first Europeans to do so. Two years later he and three other missionaries travelled up the Thames Valley. On the way there was a curious encounter with some European traders. When the two parties camped for the night near each other the mission natives started singing hymns, as was their custom. Not to be outdone the traders retaliated by rendering several choruses of "Old King Cole". On the whole it was an amicable encounter and the following morning both sets of travellers went their respective ways, rather cheered by the meeting.

In 1834 another epic journey was made, this time by the Rev. A. N. Brown and James Hamlin, who set out from the Bay of Islands to the unknown Waikato region. The two missionaries managed to reach Kaipara but were unable to find guides to take them farther, and rather than paddle their canoes against the current up the Kaipara River they decided to walk overland. It proved to be a desperately hard journey over unknown tracks. They lived off the land and more than once almost gave themselves up for lost: but they and their bearers managed to stagger as far as the Waikato River, where they built a number of rafts in order to cross. They paddled down to the mouth and started walking overland again. In all, the journey occupied five months but the two men were more than satisfied; they had discovered good land and what was more important the natives had declared that they wanted a mission station opened.

Missionaries penetrated farther and farther inland, sometimes preceded by traders, often going in advance of them. The

An early church mission station on the Waikato River, New Zealand.

Wesleyans and the Catholics in their turn showed just as much enterprise and courage in opening up new paths for Christianity. Danger was a constant companion in their travels. Father John Forest, a Catholic priest, described a fairly typical incident:

> I left for Opotiki, the mission of Fathers Comte and Reignier; after a two days' trip, we arrived at the entrance to the port at sunset. To get in, there is a bar to cross. Our captain lost his way, and the ship went on to a sandbank; the waves, not quite able to take us off, broke over us, and covered even the bridge every few minutes. The other travellers, most of them natives, threw themselves into the water to swim ashore; but I, who swim like a piece of lead, what was I to do? I prayed to our good mother; one is never more fervent than during circumstances such as these, and never does one realise better the weakness and helplessness of man. Mary did not abandon me. I was able, by means of a rope, to get into a small boat and arrive on Mother Earth in the midst of boiling breakers. We found ourselves on a little island, but, less fortunate than St. Paul in one of his shipwrecks, there was no-one to offer us hospitality.

In spite of adversities missionaries of all faiths continued to make progress, ever moving south from their initial position on the northern peninsula of the North Island. Increasingly they made converts, though the Maoris were at first bewildered by the proliferation of denominations, each claiming to be the one true faith. Inevitably the missions played each other down, each denomination taking every opportunity to disparage the other faiths. The Anglicans scoffed at the Wesleyans' practice of lay baptism, the Methodists in turn accused the Anglicans of being so High Church as to approach Catholicism, though both Protestant sects combined to condemn the Catholics' habit of distributing crucifixes and medallions.

Charles Darwin visited the mission station at Waimate in 1835 and rhapsodised over the farm buildings, the fields and the houses of the European missionaries, and went on to describe the crops:

> . . . fine crops of barley and wheat in full ear, and others of potatoes and of clover . . . but I cannot attempt to describe all I saw; there were large gardens, with every fruit and vegetable which England produces, and many belonging to a warmer

The Rev. John Waterhouse superintending the landing of the Rev. Charles Creed at Taranaki (New Zealand), 1841. From a painting in oils by Baxter; a woodcut of this painting appeared in the Wesleyan Missionary Notices January 1845, with a detailed description, part of which reads: "Seven native females in a transport of joy, anxiously carrying Mrs Creed, with the greatest care, to the shore."

climate. I may instance asparagus, kidney beans, cucumbers, rhubarb, apples and pears, figs, peaches, apricots, grapes, olives, gooseberries, currants, hops, gorse for fences, and English oaks! and many different kinds of flowers.

Some of the early missionaries, before the Church Missionary Society expressed disapproval of Henry Williams's alleged land speculations, purchased a great deal of land on their own account, running in some instances to thousands of acres. This sort of transaction was viewed with disfavour by the traders, who objected to being preached at by men who seemed in some cases to be as deeply immersed in commerce as themselves.

By the middle of the century the missionaries had converted many Maoris and were on their way to converting many more. In the process the Maoris were to lose many of their customs and traditions, and to become involved in a large-scale war with the Europeans. The white men were to come to their country in ever-increasing numbers. Like most native races in the Pacific the Maoris wondered if any benefit had been brought to them by the introduction of the white man and his civilisation.

In the second half of the nineteenth century in Australia most of the emphasis in church work lay in establishing the different denominations and catering for the vastly swollen European population. The country was also used as the headquarters of various missions in the Pacific islands, notably the Melanesian Mission and the Methodist Board of Missions. Some devoted missionaries tried to bring Christianity to the Aborigines — when they could find them. For the greater part, however, the Aborigines were ignored by the Churches, some of whom genuinely believed that it would be impossible to convert them, an attitude that led John G. Paton, on a visit to Australia in 1863, to comment tartly:

Recall, ere you read further, what the Gospel has done for the near kindred of these same Aboriginals. On our own Aneityum 3,500 Cannibals have been led to renounce their heathenism, and are leading a civilized and Christian life. In Fiji, 70,000 Cannibals have been brought under the influence of the Gospel; and 13,000 members of the Churches are professing to live and work for Jesus. In Samoa, 34,000 Cannibals have professed Christianity; and in nineteen years, its College has sent forth 206 Native teachers and evangelists. On our New Hebrides, more than 12,000 Cannibals have been brought to sit at the feet of Christ, though I mean not to say that they are all model Christians; and 133 of the Natives have been trained and sent forth as teachers and preachers of the Gospel. Had Christ been brought in the same way into the heart and life of the Aborigines by the Christians of Australia and of Britain — equally blessed results would as surely have followed, for He is the same yesterday, to-day, and for ever.

Some efforts were made in this direction, and missions worked among the labourers in the sugarfields of Queensland towards the end of the century, but there was a great deal in what Paton said. In the case of the Aborigines of Australia the Church had missed a great opportunity.

10

THE HEAT OF THE DAY

Throughout the South Pacific men and women of all faiths and colours are continuing the work started by the pioneer missionaries. No-one who has seen them at their task could fail to realise that theirs is an onerous, never-ending and often desperately lonely job, one that could be carried out only by people of great courage and dedication. In peace and war they have brought faith, comfort, succour, education and medicine to hundreds of thousands of islanders over the years. Nor is their work always appreciably easier than that of their predecessors. The climate is enervating and the conditions in which they live often primitive. Among the smaller islands their main means of transport remain tiny vessels and walking. Though most of the area is Christian, there are still tracts of pagan territory. Parts of Papua-New Guinea have yet to be evangelised, and as recently as the 1960s a missionary was murdered on Malaita in the Solomons.

Yet it cannot be denied that the groundwork for the propagation of the gospel was laid by the missionaries of the nineteenth century and the closing decade of the eighteenth century. These were the men and woman who, both literally and metaphorically, toiled in the heat of the day to bring Christianity to the islands of the Pacific.

They had their detractors. Some of them were scoffed at for attempting to bring to the islands the manners and customs of a Birmingham suburb. Others were accused of taking every opportunity of feathering their own nests, engaging in trading ventures and land speculation. There were those who succumbed to the temptations of a languorous, permissive society. A few fled back to the culture that they knew and appreciated. For some the exercise of power proved too attractive. Most missionaries at one time or aonther were accused of interfering in matters that did not concern them.

There are elements of truth in all these charges. There were black sheep among the early missionaries as well as martyrs and heroes. Yet there is little doubt that the missionaries contributed greatly to the welfare of the islands and the islanders and that the good they did far outweighed any harm. While it is arguable that it might have been better for the islanders had white men never come to the Pacific, once they had arrived it needed the calming, temperate presence of the men of God to combat the worst excesses of the unscrupulous soldiers-of-fortune. It was the missionaries who educated the islanders, showed them how to trade and hold their own in the new economic circumstances. The missionaries taught the islanders skills and crafts, brought them medicine and medical attention, showed them how to live a better, healthier life. They put an end to cannibalism, infanticide, the slaughter of widows, and blood-feuds.

The missionaries, too, were always present to stir the government in Britain to protect the islanders. By the end of the nineteenth century, and for some years before, the Christian missions formed an extremely potent pressure group. They remained a constant brake on some Europeans who otherwise would have raped and plundered unchecked among the islands. They helped to limit the depredations of the slave-traders. They brought law and order to the Pacific long before any established governments were able to do so. Nor were the missionaries afraid to oppose authority when they thought it right. Most of the societies, for example, combined to combat any widespread colonialism in the Pacific.

The main aim of the missionaries was to bring the word of God to the islanders and to convert them to Christianity but there were many other intentions only a little less important. They wanted to improve the living conditions of the islanders and to broaden their horizons; this has been true of evangelists the world over, as I. J. Merle Davis has pointed out in *New Buildings on Old Foundations* (International Missionary Council, 1945), when writing of the monks in the Middle Ages:

The Way of Christ called for better and nobler living and so the monks made of their monastic establishment little islands of Christian culture, activity and worship where such a way of life could be demonstrated. The monks cleared the land, tilled the soil, introduced new varieties of grain, vegetables and fruit trees. They brought cattle, sheep, hogs, and poultry. They introduced fish and bee culture. They built looms for textiles,

"A village in Pukapuka, under heathenism."

"The same village, under Christianity," Pukapuka, or Danger Island, is one of the Cook Islands. From *Life in the Southern Isles*, by the Rev. William Wyatt Gill, the Religious Tract Society, London.

tanned hides, made bricks and blew glass. They puddled, poured and moulded iron. They planted vineyards for wine and made cheese, butter, candles and soap. Along with the farming, stock-raising and artisan trades went the practice of medicine and training in silver and goldsmith work, weaving, embroidery, painting, illuminating and music. These industries and arts were needed for the furnishing and maintenance of the church and monastery but their practice passed on to the community which clustered around them an appreciation of better and gentler ways of living together with the skills required for following them. It is important to note that the monks did not bring a program of economic and social uplift into the wilderness for its own sake, but that the culture-building activities emanated from and were organised around a Christian church. Wherever they settled, the monks also established schools, not only to train the novitiates for the Church, but to educate the children of the countryside. . . . Through this wide program of activities, the monasteries laid the foundations of civilization in western Europe.

As with the monks in medieval Europe, so too, to a great extent with the first missionaries in the Pacific. Sometimes the missionaries were mistaken, impatient or tactless. With the passing of time they grew more accustomed to the customs and *tabus* of the islands and to adjust their teaching to them. By their own example the majority of missionaries showed the islanders how Christian men and women conducted themselves in good times and bad. The results of their pilgrim efforts may be seen in ten thousand or so Pacific island villages today.

BIBLIOGRAPHY

Alexander, Gilchrist, *From the Middle Temple to the South Seas,* Murray, London, 1927.

Amherst, Lord and Thomson, B., *The Discovery of the Solomon Islands,* Hakluyt Society, London, 1901.

Anderson, the Rev. Rufus, *The Hawaiian Islands: Their Progress and Condition Under Missionary Labours,* Gould and Lincoln, Boston, 1864.

Armstrong, S., *The Melanesian Mission,* Ibister, London, 1887.

Baker, J. R., *Man and Animals in the New Hebrides,* Routledge, London, 1927.

Barrow, Sir John, *The Eventful History of the Mutiny and Piratical Seizure of H.M.S. 'Bounty': Its Cause and Consequences,* 2nd ed., John Murray, London, 1835.

Bartlett, Samuel, *Historical Sketch of the Hawaiian Mission, and the Missions to Micronesia and the Marquesas Islands,* Boston, 1869.

Beaglehole, J. C., *The Exploration of the Pacific,* A. & C. Black, London, 1934.

Belcher, Sir Edward, *Narrative of a Voyage round the World, performed in Her Majesty's Ship 'Sulphur' during the years 1836-1842,* Colburn, London, 1843.

Belshaw, C. S., *Island Administration in the South-West Pacific,* Oxford, 1950.

Bingham, Hiram, *A Residence of Twenty-One Years in the Sandwich Islands,* Huntingdon, Hartford, 1847.

Brenchley, J. L., *Jottings During the Cruise of H.M.S. 'Curacao' among the South Sea Islands in 1865,* Longmans, Green, London, 1873.

Burtt, J., *Reminiscences Re George Augustus Selwyn DD,* Brett, Auckland, 1907.

Buzacott, Rev. Aaron, *Mission Life in the Islands of the Pacific,* Snow, London, 1886.

Campbell, the Rev. John, *The Martyr of Erromanga,* Snow, London, 1842.

Carrington, Hugh, *The Discovery of Tahiti,* Hakluyt Society, London, 1948.

Cheesman, Evelyn, *Backwaters of the Savage South Seas,* Jarrolds, London, 1933.

Cheever, the Rev. Henry, *Life in the Sandwich Islands,* Bentley, London, 1851.

Choules, J. and Smith, T., *The Origin and History of Missions,* Boston, 1842.

Churchward, W. B., *Blackbirding in the South Pacific,* Swan Sonnenschien, London, 1888.

Churchward, W. B., *My Consulate in Samoa,* Bentley, London, 1887.

Codrington, R. H., *The Melanesians,* Oxford, The Clarendon Press, Oxford, 1891.

Colwell, J., *A Century in the Pacific,* Kelly, London, 1914.

Coome, Florence, *Islands of Enchantment: Many-sided Melanesia,* Macmillan, London, 1911.

Coote, Walter, *The Western Pacific, 1875-1881,* Sampson Low, London, 1883.

Coulter, J., *Adventures in the Pacific,* Curry, Dublin, 1845.

Davidson, J. W., *Samoa mo Samoa,* Oxford University Press, Melbourne, 1967.

Dalrymple, A., *An Account of the Discoveries made in the South Pacific Ocean Previous to 1764,* London, 1767.

Dillon, P., *Narrative of a Voyage in the South Seas,* Hirst Chance, London, 1829.

Dyson, the Rev. M., *My Story of Samoan Methodism,* Fergusson & Moore, Melbourne, 1875.

Elkington, E. W. and Handy, N. H., *The Savage South Seas,* Black, London, 1907.

Ellis, John, *Life of William Ellis,* Murray, London, 1873.

Ellis, William, *Polynesian Researches,* Fisher & Jackson, London, 1839.

Ellis, William, *History of the London Missionary Society,* London, 1844.

Erskine, J. E., *Journal of a Cruise among the Islands in the Western Pacific in Her Majesty's Ship 'Havannah',* Murray, London, 1853.

Fox, C. E., *The Threshold of the Pacific,* Kegan Paul, London, 1924.

Fox, C. E., *Lord of the Southern Isles,* Mowbray, London, 1958.

Geddie, J., *The Story of Aneityum,* Nova Scotia, 1875.

Gill, the Rev. W., *Gems from the Coral Islands,* Ward, London, 1856.

Goodenough, J. G., *Journals of Commander Goodenough,* King, London, 1876.

Gordon, the Rev. G. N., *The Last Martyrs of Erromanga,* Halifax, 1863.

Grimshaw, Beatrice, *From Fiji to the Cannibal Islands,* Nelson, London, 1907.

Gunn, W., *The Gospel in Futuna,* Hodder & Stoughton, London, 1914.

Cuppy, H. B., *The Solomon Islands and their Natives,* Swan Sonnenschein, London, 1887.

Haldane, C., *Tempest Over Tahiti,* Constable, London, 1963.

Harrison, Tom, *Savage Civilisation,* Gollancz, London, 1937.

Hope, J. L. A., *In Quest of Coolies,* King, London, 1872.

How, F. D., *Bishop John Selwyn, A Memoir,* Isbister, London, 1900.

Inglis, J., *In the New Hebrides,* Nelson, London, 1887.

Johnson, Martin, *Cannibal Island,* Houghton Mifflin, Boston, 1922.

Kay, J., *Slave Trade in the New Hebrides,* Edmonston & Douglas, Edinburgh, 1872.

Kuykendall, R. S., *The Hawaiian Kingdom, 1778-1854,* University of Hawaii Press, Honolulu, 1948.

Lamb, Robert, *Saints and Savages,* Blackwood, Edinburgh, 1905.

Lamont, E. H., *Wild Life among the Pacific Islanders,* Hurst & Blackett, London, 1867.

Langridge, A. K., *The Conquest of Cannibal Tanna*, Hodder & Stoughton, London, 1934.

Lawry, Rev. W., *Missions in the Tonga and Feejee Islands*, Lane & Scott, New York, 1852.

Lovett, R., *The History of the London Missionary Society, 1795-1895*, Frowde, London, 1899.

Lynch, Bohun, *Isles of Illusion*, Constable, London, 1923.

Mackaness, G., *Life of Vice-Admiral William Bligh*, Sydney, 1931.

Markham, A. H., *The Cruise of the 'Rosario'*, Sampson Low, London, 1873.

Markham, Sir Clements, *The Voyages of Pedro Fernandez de Quiros, 1595 to 1606*, Hakluyt Society, London, 1904.

Martin, K. L. P., *Missionaries and Annexation in the Pacific*, Oxford University Press, Oxford, 1924.

Maude, H. E., *Of Islands and Men*, O.U.P., Melbourne, 1968.

Morrell, W. P., *Britain in the Pacific Islands*, O.U.P., Clarendon Press, 1960.

Moss, Frederick J., *Through Atolls and Islands in the Great South Sea*, Sampson Low, London, 1889.

Murray, the Rev. A. W., *Forty Years Mission Work in Polynesia and New Guinea, from 1835 to 1875*, Nisbet, London, 1876.

Nicolson, R. B., *The Pitcairners*, London, 1965.

Palmer, George, *Kidnapping in the South Seas*, Edmonston & Douglas, Edinburgh, 1871.

Paton, J., *John G. Paton*, London, 1898.

Pritchard, W. T., *Polynesian Reminiscences*, Chapman & Hall, London, 1866.

Prout, E., *Memoirs of the Life of the Rev. John Williams*, Snow, London, 1843.

Scarr, Deryck, *Fragments of Empire: A History of the Western Pacific High Commission, 1877-1914*, Canberra, 1967.

Sharp, C. A., *Ancient Voyagers in the Pacific*, Polynesian Society, Wellington, 1956.

Shineberg, Dorothy, *They Came for Sandalwood*, Melbourne University Press, Melbourne, 1967.

Steel, the Rev. R., *The New Hebrides and Christian Missions*, Nisbet, London, 1880.

Stock, Eugene, *The History of the Church Missionary Society, Its Environment, Its Men and Its Work*, Church Missionary Society, London, 1899.

Thomson, Sir Basil, *The Diversions of a Prime Minister*, Blackwood, Edinburgh, 1894.

Turner, the Rev. G., *Nineteen Years in Polynesia*, Snow, London, 1861.

Veeson, George, *An Authentic Narartive of Four Years' Residence at Tongataboo*, Longman, London, 1810.

Ward, J. M., *British Policy in the South Pacific, 1786-1893*, Australian Publishing Co., Sydney, 1948.

Watsford, the Rev. G., *Glorious Gospel Triumphs*, Kelly, London, 1900.

West, the Rev. James, *Ten Years in South-Central Polynesia,* London, 1865.

Williams, John, *A Narrative of Missionary Enterprises in the South Sea Islands,* Snow, London, 1837.

Wilson, W., *A Missionary Voyage to the South Pacific,* Chapman, London, 1799.

Wright, Louis B. and Fry, Mary Isabel, *Puritans in the South Seas,* Holt, New York, 1936.

INDEX